MYLES MUNROE

APPLYING THE
KINGDOM

DESTINY IMAGE® PUBLISHERS, INC.
P.O. Box 310, Shippensburg, PA 17257-0310

*"Speaking to the Purposes of God for this Generation
and for the Generations to Come."*

BAHAMAS FAITH MINISTRY
P.O. Box N9583
Nassau, Bahamas

This book and all other Destiny Image, Revival Press, Mercy Place, Fresh Bread, Destiny Image Fiction, and Treasure House books are available at Christian bookstores and distributors worldwide.

For a U.S. bookstore nearest you, call 1-800-722-6774.
For more information on foreign distributors, call 717-532-3040.
Or reach us on the Internet: www.destinyimage.com

Hardcover ISBN 10: 0-7684-2489-5
ISBN 13: 978-0-7684-2489-8

Paperback ISBN 10: 0-7684-2597-2
ISBN 13: 978-0-7684-2597-0

For Worldwide Distribution, Printed in the U.S.A.

Hard Cover 1 2 3 4 5 6 7 8 9 10 11 / 09 08 07
Paperback 1 2 3 4 5 6 7 8 9 10 11 / 09 08 07

CONTENTS

PREFACE

The number one priority of humanity is material security. Pop singer Madonna made it to the top of the music hit charts with a song, "Material Girl," that did not make much logical sense. The song sold millions of copies around the world including the United States, Europe, Africa, South America, Canada, Japan and the Caribbean, and stayed on the top of the charts for weeks.

The question that must be asked is why did this seemingly unimportant subject attract so many people, both young and old? I believe this phenomenon was due to the fact that the lyrics of this simple song captured the spirit of the age and the preoccupation of our and all generations. Many adults who may not agree with the personality, lifestyle, philosophy, or musical genre of the pop culture cannot deny the truth this song expresses.

The entire world seems to turn on the axis of materialism. Whether one lives in the shadows of poverty of the industrial concrete jungle in the economic capitals of the world, or sits on the corporate boards of Fortune 500 companies located on the 60th floor of an executive building, or lives in a Third World country village, the allure of materialism generates a magnetic field which causes people to sacrifice any and everything to obtain it.

The older generations of the world's nations pursue material goods at the expense of personal health, family, marriages, wholesome morality and values, and spiritual sensitivity. They build houses too big for families they lose; buy expensive cars to drive to a job where they spend 16 hours a day; they buy designer clothing that gathers dust in the closet; and, they join country clubs they have no time to enjoy.

Many sacrifice their loved ones on the altar of temporary pleasure and join the rat race in hopes of becoming the "big rat." Others purchase second homes they never live in and buy complicated adult toys they never use.

Still others provide heaps of material goods for their children who have no appreciation for the value or cost of the goods, and apply the culture of "use and toss" reducing the spirit of gratitude among the young. What a material tragedy. It seems as if the philosophy of this generation is founded in the belief that one's value, self-worth, self-esteem and self-concept is derived not from who they are but from what they possess. Their life is measured by the things they accumulate not who they are. They fail to understand that we don't need *things* to have life, we need *life* to have things.

Even more staggering are the children and youth of this older generation. The culture of materialism is the driving force of life for youth worldwide. The worlds of fashion, music, sports, education, social status, and careers are all driven by materialism. The explosion of the music-video industry promoting the image of riches and affluence flaunted by young men and women who portray no record of an honest day's work further compounds the idea that success in life is measured in terms of material wealth.

The success of television shows like "Lifestyles of the Rich and Famous" strike a deep cord in the psyche of our materialistic culture and draws on the hidden aspiration of millions to pursue material wealth.

This preoccupation with materialism is also the source of much of the criminal activity within many communities of our nations and manifests itself in anti-social scourges such as the illegal drug industry, gangs, prostitution, robberies, and corruption in corporate and political regions. The hypnotic power of "material things" has controlled mankind from the days of the early Egyptian civilization and can be traced throughout the human journey history. Warnings against this controlling power can be found in writings as far back as Moses and Kings David and Solomon of Israel.

Renowned behavioral scientist and psychologist Abraham Maslow did extensive researched on the subject of human motivation, and concluded that all of the 6.7 billion humans on planet Earth are motivated by primarily by the same needs and are willing to pursue the meeting of these needs at all cost. His list of human priority needs include: food, water, clothing, shelter, housing, and security.

Over 2,000 years ago the greatest teacher of all time, Jesus Christ, presented His list of human priority and admonished mankind to consider these material priorities. One of His students, Matthew, recorded these words by His master teacher while addressing this subject of the priority of human motivation:

> *Therefore I tell you, do not worry about your life, what you will eat or drink; or about your body, what you will wear. Is not life more important than food, and the body more important than clothes? So do not worry, saying, "What shall we eat?" or "What shall we drink?" or "What shall we wear?"* (Matthew 6:25,31).

His admonition for humanity to move their primary focus from material needs and place it on what he calls the "more important" matters of life is a startling contrast to our current global culture.

In this book I explore this repositioning of priority and the philosophy behind it. I present the solution to this debilitating possession by and preoccupation with the lure of materialism, and provide practical principles designed to free us all from the self-destructive and socially abusing spirit of materialism.

Let's journey together and discover the Creator's original priority, and embrace the opportunity to rearrange our life's priorities to experience stress-free living above circumstances and measures of temporal success.

INTRODUCTION

The wise person questions himself, the fool others.
                                    —Henry Arnold

In the depth of every human soul on earth is a search for meaning, purpose, significance and value. No matter what race, culture, language, or religion, this preoccupation with the need to find answers to our existence is inherent in every human spirit.

For what are we searching? Why is this internal search so common among all humankind? Could it be that this common search is evidence of a common loss? What did we lose and where did we lose it? Where can we and will we ever find it? It is my belief that every person on earth is searching for what the Father of all humankind lost—dominion over earth.

Most people don't know what they are searching for. They know they are searching for something, some purpose that will give meaning and fulfillment to their lives, but they cannot identify what it is. Many seek an answer in the pursuit of money, power, possessions, or pleasure. Others search for it in science, philosophy, or intellectualism. Some turn to alcohol or consciousness-altering drugs.

There are also those who look to religion for the meaning of life. In every case, the result is the same. No matter how hard they try or how diligently they search, the object of their quest eludes them. Despite their best efforts, the answer they seek remains hidden from view. After all, it is extremely difficult to find something when you do not know what you are looking for!

All of us, essentially, are restless at the very core of our being. This is because each of us has a built-in drive to rule and dominate, to exercise control over our circumstances and environment. Yet, very few of us experience this in reality. For the vast majority of us, the opposite is true: our circumstances and environment control us. Something deep inside of us yearns for mastery and fulfillment that seem to be just outside our reach, as if we were meant for a destiny different than the one we are living. It is as though we long to return to a place we once inhabited, but lost somewhere along the way; and now we have no idea how to get back. The majority of humans lead lives of quiet desperation.

This is, indeed, the exact plight of humanity. Each of us is tailor-made for rulership. Our Designer and Manufacturer built into us both the inclination and the capability for exercising dominion over the natural order. Our original destiny was to rule as kings and queens on the earth as vice-regents of our Creator, the King of Heaven. In this way we would extend the government, authority, and influence of His invisible supernatural realm into the visible realm of the natural world.

That destiny was altered, however, when the first human pair abdicated to a usurper and pretender to the throne, an unemployed cherub who arrogantly ascended to the place of earthly authority designed and reserved for man. Our deepest heart cry ever since, although unidentified by most of us, has been to return to that place of dominion our original human ancestors once enjoyed. We long to find what they lost.

"The greatest failure in life is being successful in the wrong assignment."

CHAPTER ONE

FIRST THINGS FIRST

THE KEYS TO LIFE

Every human is searching for the simple formula to a successful, fulfilled life. They want to find the one key that unlocks the door to the good life and answers the questions of their heart. Perhaps this is why *The Secret* became a sudden best-selling book even though its reign was short lived. This book promised the final key to life and success. (I was amazed to find when I read this book, that is was simply a restatement of all the principles already written in the Bible, and the same material I and many others have been sharing for years. In essence, *the secret* was never a secret.)

If you conducted a sidewalk poll in any city, anywhere in the world, and asked people, "What is the key to life?" you would get many different answers. Some would say the key to life is to make as much money as you can, as quickly as you can, and to hold onto it as long as you can. Others would see gaining political power and influence as the key to life. Love would be the key for many.

Then there are always those who would say that there is no key to life. Life is an accident; it just happened and therefore has no key or significance. The fact is, most people don't know the key to life. This is why so many people live tragic lives; they don't know why they are here. They haven't a clue about how to make their time on this earth count for something worthwhile. Their existence is, in many ways, a kind of "living death," because a life without purpose is not really a life at all.

So what is the key to life? Finding your true purpose and living it. I know the word *purpose* has been almost over-used in recent years and many think they understand it, but I wish to advise that this most essential component in life has never and can never be exhausted. Let me sum this up in four statements that all relate to purpose— four "keys" to understanding the difference between a purpose-filled life and a life with no meaning.

*The greatest **tragedy** in life is not death, but life without a purpose.* Many people today are obsessed with finding ways to prolong their lives. They are so caught up with trying to live longer that they never stop to consider why they are living at all. Drifting from one day to the next without purpose, with untapped potential and unfulfilled dreams; this is for many a fate worse than death. The rising suicide rate in modern society bears this truth out. Many people, bereft of hope, take their own lives because they find death more appealing than continuing what is to them a meaningless existence. Finding our purpose in life is critically important.

Second, *the greatest **challenge** in life is knowing what to do.* We get up every day and go about our daily activities, but are we doing what we are supposed to be doing? With all the options and choices that lie before us every day, that can be a difficult question to answer. Do you know what to do with your life? What drive gets you out of bed every morning? What purpose propels you through each day? Are you living for a paycheck? Or are you living for a purpose? With each passing day you grow older and use up more of your time and energy. Are you doing what you are supposed to be doing? Do you even know what to do? These are tough questions, but learning the answers is vital to your future.

Next, *the greatest **mistake** in life is being busy, but not effective.* Being busy is a common human pastime. But just because you're busy doesn't mean that what you're doing is worth doing. Many people deceive themselves into believing that being busy all the time gives their lives significance. Significance has nothing to do with busyness but everything to do with effectiveness. Jesus of Nazareth was the most effective person who ever lived but He was never busy. Everything Jesus did had purpose. He knew what He was supposed to do and did it, and that made Him effective. It is a tragedy to waste time and energy on unfocused busyness because those resources, once expended, can never be regained. We must learn how to live effectively without being busy.

And finally, *the greatest **failure** in life is being successful in the wrong assignment.* Success alone is not enough; you must succeed in the right thing. Sincerity alone is not enough because you can be sincerely wrong. Faithfulness alone is not enough because you can be faithful to the wrong faith. Commitment alone is not enough because you can be committed to the wrong cause. Succeeding in the wrong assignment is failure.

If a teacher gives you a test and instructs you to answer only the odd-numbered questions, and you answer the even-numbered questions instead, even if you answer every question correctly you will still fail because you didn't follow instructions. You succeeded in the wrong assignment, which means you failed. God is not impressed with our sincerity, faithfulness, commitment, or success unless we are pursuing the right assignment—His assignment. Anything else is failure.

ESTABLISHING PRIORITIES: THE SECRET TO SUCCESS

As any successful person will tell you, one of the fundamental keys to success in any field of endeavor is learning to establish priorities and then living by them. Any activity that does not fit into or advance any of those priorities is put on the backburner or even eliminated, even if that activity is good in and of itself. Even good activities, if they are incompatible with our established priorities, can become unnecessary distractions that hinder our progress toward success. A priority is the principal thing upon which we place our primary focus. It is that thing we consider to be of highest value and worth, first among all others. Establishing priorities means ranking everything in order of importance, determining which is most important, and then focusing our time, attention, and energy there. It is a matter of putting first things first.

Essentially, our success boils down to the issue of how efficiently and effectively we use our time. Learning to establish priorities, or to put first things first, is a critical key to effective time management. Most of us are busy people for whom time is at a premium. Remember, however, that busyness does not necessarily mean effectiveness. Successful people are effective people because they know how to set priorities. Priorities help us avoid distractions, focus on the most important things, and get the most value out of our time every day.

Success in life is the effective use of time. Each of us is the sum total of what we spend our time on. The person you are today is a result of how you have used your time in the past. If you are overweight, for example, it may be because you have spent too much time sitting around eating and watching television, and not enough time exercising and being active in other ways. If you are ignorant and lacking in knowledge, you may be spending time on aimless and unproductive activities that would be better spent reading books or going to school. The way you invest your time determines the level of your success.

We need to pay close attention to time because *time is the true measure of life.* Our life on earth is essentially human consciousness residing in a physical body that exists in a linear but finite continuum of time and space. In the life to come, in eternity, time will not be a factor, but now it is. In our physical existence we are bound by the constraints of time.

Time is also the currency of life. Currency is the medium of exchange used in an economy to purchase goods and services. Just as money is the currency of an economy, time is the currency of life. And just as we use money to purchase things, we use time to purchase life. Financial success always involves the wise investment of money to get the biggest possible return for the smallest outlay. In the same way, success in life means receiving the greatest returns and benefits—to ourselves as well as to others—for the time invested. Every morning we all wake up with the same amount of time currency: 24 hours. Where we go and how high we rise in life depend on how we spend and invest that irreplaceable currency.

It stands to reason, then, that *how we spend our time determines the quality of our life **and** death.* How will people feel when you die? Will they be sad...or relieved? The way you invest your time this side of the grave will make the difference. Our quality of life (and that of the people closest to us) is directly related to how we spend our currency of time. We will be healthy, wealthy, wise, and spiritually mature in direct proportion to the time we invest in these things. In a very real sense we become what we spend our time on. Time is a precious commodity that must be carefully and wisely invested.

Because time is currency and a precious commodity, it should come as no surprise to discover that *everything and everyone is after our time.* Modern life is a constant bombardment of voices, ideas, opinions, causes, and expectations, from people in every degree of acquaintance, all vying for our time and attention. Some of it is worthwhile and deserves our attention; most of it does not.

How do we tell the difference? This is where establishing priorities comes in. Without clear priorities, we run the danger of wasting precious time listening to the wrong voices or allowing ourselves to be drawn in the wrong direction.

Knowing your priorities will help you evaluate the voices pulling at you and identify those that are the most important. The best way to minimize confusion is to get into the habit of deciding beforehand how you will spend your time each day. Personally, I plan out my time and focus for each day the day before. I have found that knowing where I am headed as I go into each day helps me avoid unnecessary distractions along the way. You can't give your time or attention to every competing voice, so let your priorities help you zero in on those that are the most important. Let the others go.

Coming full circle, then, we see that the key to success is effective use of time, and *the key to effective use of time is correct priorities.* The only way to spend your time currency effectively is to identify the correct priorities for your life. If you do not know what you are supposed to do, where you are supposed to go, or how you are going to get there, you are in constant danger of abusing your currency and allowing others to do the same. Take it from me, nothing is more rewarding than to wake up in the morning knowing exactly what to do and knowing that what you are doing is right and correct.

Notice that I did not use the word "good." Good is not always right. Many times we end up abusing our currency because we are distracted by good things that take the place of right things, thereby causing us to be busy, but not effective.

God is not impressed with busyness. The only way to live effectively is to use your time on the correct priorities for your life. Some of your priorities may be good, but not correct. It is important to learn the difference. Time wasted on incorrect priorities is currency that is gone forever. It can never be regained.

THE PRIORITY OF PRIORITY

In addition to helping us use our time effectively, there are numerous other significant reasons why establishing priorities should be a priority for us. For one thing, *preoccupation with priority preserves and protects life.* What is life? Time. And what is priority? Doing the right thing at the right time in the right way. Priority will protect your life because doing the right thing at the right time in the right way keeps us from doing the wrong thing at the wrong time in the wrong way. Priority enables us to spend our days putting first things first.

Second, *correct priority is the principle of progress.* True progress is measured not by how much we get done but by whether or not we are moving in the right direction. We may accomplish many good things, but if we are focused on the wrong things, we will not make any progress toward our true goal.

If I set out to drive from Daytona Beach, Florida, north to Jacksonville, but end up heading south toward Miami, I may "progress" many miles, but in the wrong direction. I will never reach my intended objective. Movement is not necessarily a sign of progress any more than busyness is a sign of effectiveness.

It's important to move in the right direction, and that means finding God's priority. Aligning ourselves with God's priority ensures that we will always travel in the right direction in life. And what is God's priority? *Kingdom first!*

Correct priority also protects time. As we saw earlier, knowing and doing what is most important helps us avoid abusing time and wasting that precious currency.

In addition to protecting time, *correct priority also protects energy.* When our lives are correctly prioritized, we can afford to exert our energy with confidence because we know we are using it effectively, correctly, and for the right purpose. We should strive not to be busy but to be correct. Our energy and God's priority are too important for us to wake up one morning and realize that everything we have done for the last ten or twenty years was wrong! Correct priorities give us the energy to put first things first—to seek first the Kingdom of God and His righteousness.

A fifth reason for focusing on priorities: *correct priority protects talents and gifts.* Knowing your priorities will help you avoid expending your talents and gifts on unimportant or unworthy endeavors. Most people today use their gifts and abilities in the pursuit of selfish and worldly goals that have nothing to do with the Kingdom of Heaven. Their top priority is gratifying their own desires. However, even good and honorable pursuits can become a problem if they distract us from other endeavors that are more important.

Imagine looking back from the autumn years of your life and realizing that you wasted your gifts and talents on the wrong things, never accomplishing what you were put here on earth to do. What a tragedy that would be! Establishing correct priorities in your life now will help ensure that never happens. Correct priorities means God's priority, and God's priority is *Kingdom first!* With God's priority in place as your priority, you can pursue life with confidence and no fear of later regret.

Correct priority also protects decisions. Once you know what your priorities are, decision making becomes very easy because you understand not only what you should be doing but also what you should not be doing. This gives you confidence to say no to requests, even honorable ones that would distract you from your primary focus. Every decision you make either helps or hinders you in fulfilling your life purpose. Unless you know the priorities of your life, you have no guidelines to help you make the correct choice. Setting your heart on God's priority will enable you to choose the right course and maximize your life's effectiveness.

Along with decision making, *correct priority protects discipline.* People without priorities usually are undisciplined people. Since they do not know which direction to go, they shoot out in every direction, following every whim, going nowhere, and dissipating any possible effectiveness they could have. Establishing correct priorities injects automatic discipline into your life because it gives your life a sharp and narrow focus with laser-like intensity. Priority-induced discipline protects you from wasting your time, energy, effort, talents, gifts and, especially, your life.

Every year I receive over 700 invitations from around the world to speak; and I must say no to at least 600 of them. How do I choose which ones to accept and which ones to decline? Simple—I know my priorities. It is easy to say no when you know what yes is. Having correct priorities takes the guesswork out of decision making and discipline.

This brings us to the final point for the importance of priority: *correct priority simplifies life.* If you want your life to become simple, simply find out what your priorities should be and live accordingly. That's really all there is to it. The young country preacher, Jesus Christ, lived life more effectively than all others, yet His life was very simple.

What was the secret to His amazingly effective life? He reduced all of life to two simple pursuits: (1) a Kingdom from a place called Heaven, and (2) a concept He called righteousness. In fact for the entire duration of His earthly ministry He focused only on these two subjects and related all of His principles, precepts, laws, and instructions to them.

He had only one message—the Kingdom of Heaven and righteousness—and He promised that those who made this pursuit their priority would lead a full, successful, and satisfied life. The majority of those who claim to represent Him do not promote the message He taught, and many have never considered it. It is hardly ever heard from the pulpits or the classrooms of the educational institutions that claim to train professional speakers and ministers to represent Him.

I strongly admonish and encourage you as you read the rest of this work, to take time to read the record of His life and ministry on earth found in the four Gospels of the biblical New Testament. I am certain you will be amazed and perhaps shocked to discover His original message and focus.

Time after time Jesus said, "The Kingdom of Heaven is like...the Kingdom of Heaven is like...the Kingdom of Heaven is like." Without a doubt, the Kingdom was His priority and He instructed that it must be ours too. His priority was never religion or rituals, but the introduction of a heavenly Kingdom to the earth realm.

We tend to prioritize our lives around things: food, drink, clothing, a paycheck, a car, a house. A lack in any of these areas causes us to become stressed-out and fearful, and our prayers start to focus almost exclusively on our needs. Jesus, however, tells us not to worry about these things because our heavenly Father knows that we need them (see Matt. 6:31-32). Instead, Jesus says, *"Seek first His kingdom and His righteousness, and all these things will be given to you as well"* (Matt. 6:33). In other words, if we take care of God's priority—His Kingdom—He will take care of ours.

The Kingdom of Heaven was the singular focus of Jesus' life and message. It was His priority because it was His Father's priority. It was His *first* priority.

And it must be our priority as well. First things first!

PRINCIPLES

1. We each have a built-in drive to rule and dominate, to exercise control over our circumstances and environment.

2. God's highest priority is restoring the Kingdom of Heaven on earth.

3. When we understand *Kingdom first!* we will understand how to live effectively on earth.

4. The greatest *tragedy* in life is not death, but life without a purpose.

5. The greatest *challenge* in life is knowing what to do.

6. The greatest *mistake* in life is being busy, but not effective.

7. The greatest *failure* in life is being successful in the wrong assignment.

8. Success in life is the effective use of time.

9. The key to effective use of time is correct priorities.

10. Aligning ourselves with God's priority ensures that we will always travel in the right direction in life.

11. Correct priorities mean God's priority, and God's priority is *Kingdom first!*

*"Man was created to rule things;
and not to pursue things."*

CHAPTER TWO

THE DANGER
OF MISPLACED PRIORITY

Every human heart longs for a simple life. We are naturally attracted to people who exhibit a focused, purposeful, organized life and simplified lifestyle. I believe this is the fundamental attraction of millions to the man Jesus Christ. There has never been a character who displayed such a strong spirit of personal conviction, purpose, self-awareness, confidence, self-worth, and a sense of destiny as this one man. The most impacting aspect of His life was His clear sense of priority.

Jesus Christ is the most focused and single-minded person who has ever lived. His entire life on earth was dedicated to one theme—the Kingdom of Heaven. Even by the age of 12 Jesus already knew His life purpose *and priority.* When His earthly parents, relieved at finding Him in the temple in Jerusalem after searching diligently for Him for three days, chided Him for worrying them, He said, *"Why were you searching for Me? Didn't you know I had to be in my Father's house?"* (Luke 2:49). Another way to phrase the same question: *"Did you not know that I must be about My Father's business?"* (Luke 2:49 NKJV).

Already Jesus had a singular focus on His Father's priority, and He never lost sight of it.

It was, in part, this singularity of purpose and *clarity of priorities* that caused Jesus to stand out so clearly among the people of His day. Unlike Jesus, people in general have a problem putting first things first. When man lost his dominion in the Garden of Eden he also lost his sense of proper priority and purpose. In fact, all humanity wrestles with two parallel problems related to priority: either absence of priority or misplaced priority. Both carry significant consequences.

Absence of priority causes one to drift through life with no focus or sense of purpose or direction. All of one's energy and potential are dissipated by trying to shoot off in too many directions and trying to do too many things. In many cases, people with no priority become lethargic and apathetic. A dull sameness characterizes their day-to-day living.

Misplaced priority results in wasting one's life pursuing the wrong thing, carrying out the wrong assignment. People with misplaced priority may be very focused individuals, but they are focused on the wrong thing. A life absent of priority accomplishes nothing in the end, while a life of misplaced priority may succeed in many things, but not in that which is most important. Either way, the end result is a failed life.

Do you want to come to the end of your days only to look back and have to say, regretfully, "I failed"? I know I don't!

THE TRAGEDY OF ABSENT PRIORITY

Nothing is more tragic than a life without purpose. Why is purpose so important? Purpose is the source of priorities. Defining our life's priorities is extremely difficult unless we first discover and define our purpose. Purpose is defined as the original reason and intent for the creation of a thing. Therefore, purpose is the source of meaning and significance for all created things.

If purpose is not known, priorities cannot be established and nothing significant or worthwhile in life can be accomplished. In essence, if you don't why you are on planet Earth and posses a clear sense of purpose and destiny, the demand for priorities is low or nonexistent. The truth is, if you don't know where you are going, any road will take you there. Life is daily and constantly demanding of our time energy, talent, attention, and focus. Therefore, to effectively manage the everyday demands, we must know what our priorities are. No matter what we think about life, we have to live it every day and give an account of our management.

I believe the greatest challenge in life is the daily demand to choose between competing alternatives that consume our lives. If we do not have clear and correct priorities in our lives and know what we should be doing, our lives will be an exercise in futility. The absence of priority is dangerous and detrimental.

Absence of priority results, first of all, in the *wasting of time and energy*. If you're not doing the right thing at the right time, that means you are doing the wrong thing at the wrong time. But you expend the same time and energy either way. Time and energy, once spent, are gone forever. They cannot be replaced.

When priority is absent, you become *busy on the wrong things*. If you don't know what the right things are, you will end up focusing on the wrong things. These "wrong things" may not be bad or evil in themselves; they are just wrong for you because they will distract you from pursuing your life purpose.

People without priority spend their time *doing the unnecessary*. If you think about it, most of what we do on a daily basis is not really necessary. We spend most of our time sweating, fretting, and laboring over issues that, in the eternal scheme of things, are pointless. And in the meantime, the things that really matter go undone.

In a similar way, absence of priority causes people to *major on the unimportant*. If you have no priority, you end up majoring on the minors. For some reason most of us are easily distracted or enticed away from focusing on the most important matters in life to concentrate instead on peripheral issues. Proverbs 29:18a says, "*Where there is no revelation* [vision]*, the people cast off restraint.*" Priority helps us sharpen our vision so we can focus on the most important things. Without it, we have no sense of direction and are apt to pursue whatever suits our fancy at the time.

Consequently, the absence of priority results in *preoccupation with the unimportant.* Not only do we focus on the unimportant, we become preoccupied with it. We think about it, debate it, discuss it, argue about it, and have conferences on it until, by default, it becomes a de facto priority for us. But even then, it is still the *wrong* priority.

Preoccupation leads to investment, so absence of priority causes us to *invest in the less valuable.* Who would invest in something that could produce only a 10-fold return instead of something that guarantees a 100-fold return? We all invest our time and energy and money on those things that we deem most important and of greatest value. What if we're wrong? Unless we know what is truly important, it is impossible for us to invest wisely. So the end result of the absence of priority is wasted resources.

Another consequence of absent priority is *ineffective activity.* No matter how busy you are or how much you believe you are accomplishing, if you are focused on the wrong thing all your activity will count for nothing in the end. You will be ineffective because you did not do what you were supposed to do.

The first key to effectiveness is to be sure you are doing the right thing. Then invest your time, attention, energy, and resources to doing it well. Otherwise, no matter how hard you work or how hard you try, you will not succeed.

One of the most serious consequences of absent priority is that it leads to the *abuse of gifts and talents.* If you use your talent to do something that you are not supposed to do, you have wasted your talent, even if you use it well. Some of the most gifted and talented people in the world use their God-given abilities in ways He never intended, pursuing selfish desires, indulging in lust and immorality, encouraging sensuality and promoting values that are destructive to family and society. Having talent is one thing, but knowing how to make it serve the top priority in your life is a different story. Imagine being a gifted speaker proclaiming the wrong message or a talented singer singing the wrong song. It happens every day and it is a tragedy.

People with no priority in life *forfeit purpose.* Everybody has a purpose in life but most people, sadly, never discover it. Without priority in your life you will never understand your purpose and if you do not understand your purpose you will not pursue it. If you are not pursuing the purpose you were born for, then you are pursuing the wrong thing. Even if you succeed in your pursuit you have still failed because you have not fulfilled your purpose. So, absence of priority will forfeit your purpose for living.

Finally, absence of priority results in *failure.* No matter how successful you are in what you do, if you are not doing the most important thing, the thing that you are supposed to be doing, you are failing. Busy activity, sweat, and hard work are important as long as you are focused on the right assignment. However, they can never substitute for correct priority. Priorities are like river banks; they control the flow of life.

MISPLACED PRIORITY: MEETING PERSONAL NEEDS

From the beginning of the creation of the human race, the Creator established the priority of man when He commanded the man to focus on dominion over the earth. This mandate was one of kingdom rulership, management, stewardship, and governmental administration over planet Earth. It is essential to note that there was no mention of working for survival or food but only for development and fulfillment.

Priority was never a problem in the Garden of Eden. As long as Adam and Eve walked in full and open fellowship with God, their Creator, they had no worries because He provided for all their needs. Food, water, and other resources were abundant, and the perfectly temperate climate made clothing and shelter unnecessary. Daily interaction with God, purposeful work caring for the Garden, and exercising dominion over the created order filled their lives with meaning and significance.

The first family's priority was executing ruling not pursuing resources. Mankind was preoccupied with living and life and rather than making a living. In the beginning, man's priority was *ruling things* rather than *pursuing things.* Man's provision for daily living was inherent in his relationship of obedience and corporation with his Creator and the fulfillment of His plans for the earth.

All of that changed when they lost their dominion through disobedience. Evicted from the Garden and their fellowship with God broken, they had to pay attention to things they had once taken for granted, such as food, water, shelter, and even survival itself.

It was this tragic event that initiated the change in priorities for all mankind and refocused his life on daily survival. This preoccupation with temporal things like food, clothing, covering, shelter, water, and other fundamental needs for life has consumed people to this day and was announced by the Creator as evidence of the penalty of curse for man's disobedience and treason against the Kingdom government of Heaven.

Note the words of the Creator when He addressed the family of man after the act of defiance:

> *...Cursed is the ground because of you; through painful toil you will eat of it all the days of your life. It will produce thorns and thistles for you, and you will eat the plants of the field. By the sweat of your brow you will eat your food until you return to the ground, since from it you were taken; for dust you are and to dust you will return* (Genesis 3:17-19).

This legacy of need was passed from generation to generation until it became—and remains—the consuming priority of mankind.

Everything man does outside the Kingdom of Heaven is motivated by the drive to meet personal needs. This fact was clarified and documented through the work of Abraham Maslow, a 20th century behavioral scientist and psychologist.

As I pointed out in *Kingdom Principles*, the second book in this series, Dr. Maslow, after years of observation and study of human behavior, identified nine basic needs common to all people and cultures and arranged them according to priority in a "hierarchy of needs":

1. Food

2. Water

3. Clothes

4. Housing

5. Protection

6. Security

7. Preservation

8. Self-actualization

9. Significance[1]

Maslow discovered that in every culture, the driving priority was first to acquire the basic things necessary for survival, such as food, water, and shelter and protection from the elements and predators. Until these fundamental needs were secured and assured, nothing else mattered. Once basic survival was no longer an issue, more focus was given to the aesthetic needs of self-actualization and a feeling of significance. Essentially, Maslow was correct: his hierarchy of needs accurately identifies the progressive motivations that drive human culture.

Man, in his never-ending struggle for survival and significance, and separated in spirit from the God who created him, invented religion as a vehicle in his attempt to find the lost kingdom state of rulership and control earth's resources to meet his needs. A careful study of all forms of religion reveals that *all religions are designed and built on the promise of meeting needs.* Hinduism, Buddhism, Islam, Judaism, Confucianism, Scientology, Bahai, Christian Science, Spiritism, animism, humanism—you name it—they all, without exception, seek to draw followers by promising to make their lives better, improve their circumstances, give them some sense of control over their environment, and offer answers to the questions of death and the after life. To this list we must add *institutional* Christianity—Christianity in its most rigid, regulated, ritualistic, legalistic, and stratified form, is a religion run and controlled by men.

A second common characteristic of religion is that *all religions are motivated by the pleasing of deity in order to secure basic needs* (crops, weather, protection, preservation, etc). After man became separated from God because of his sin of disobedience, he began to fear that his needs would not be met. He felt all alone and that everything was up to him. So he began to worship gods of his own invention, man-made deities that were at best only the faintest shadow of the loving and provident God Adam and Eve knew in the Garden of Eden.

This is why human history is so replete with gods: the sun god, moon god, rain god, ocean god, god of war, god of sex and fertility, god of the mountain, god of the valley, etc. Man invented religion as an effort to appease fearful and unknown deities into giving him what he needs for daily life. It was a way, hopefully, of manipulating nature and controlling one's destiny. Life was harsh, grim, and full of violence. The purpose of religion was to win the good favor of the gods by being good to them and doing them favors.

Another common denominator is that *all religions have as their primary focus the needs of the worshiper,* not the needs of the worshiped. Religious people always serve and worship their gods with the ulterior motive of expecting or hoping for something good in return. Their prayers are self-centered, usually focused almost exclusively on personal needs and desires. No attention is given to the needs or desires of the deity beyond that which is necessary to appease it and persuade it to act on their behalf. In the religion of man, the purpose of the gods is to fix things.

In all religions, therefore, *religious priority in petition and prayer is for personal needs.* Let's be honest. For most of us, 99 percent of our prayers deal with what we want from God: a new job, new car, new house, enough money not only to pay the bills but also to gratify our lust for things. How often do we spare a thought for what He wants?

Religion is selfish because *all religion is driven by the priority of needs.* The promise of meeting needs is the main reason people stay in a religion. Even when a religion fails to deliver what it promises, its followers are reluctant to leave it because faith in tradition dies hard. If their religion fails to meet their expectations for this life, rather than leave, they will simply postpone their expectations for the afterlife, however they understand it.

There is no doubt that the chief priority of man is to meet his own needs. The question we need to ask is whether or not that is the *correct* priority for man. By now we all should know that it is not. Mankind in general suffers from the dual dilemma of misplaced priority and misplaced faith.

MASLOW OVERTURNED

Maslow's theory of the hierarchy of human needs illustrates the priority of man that actually motivates human behavior in the real world—a priority centered on the acquisition of things. Jesus, however, turns Maslow's list upside down. The Kingdom of Heaven is different from the kingdoms of men. From the perspective of the Kingdom of Heaven, the priorities of man—Maslow's list—are perverted. Mankind's life focus has become twisted far afield from God's original intent. Consider the words of Jesus:

Therefore I tell you, do not worry about your life, what you will eat or drink, or about your body, what you will wear. Is not life more important than food, and the body more important than clothes? Look at the birds of the air; they do not sow or reap or store away in barns, yet your heavenly Father feeds them. Are you not much more valuable than they? Who of you by worrying can add a single hour to his life?

And why do you worry about clothes? See how the lilies of the field grow. They do not labor or spin. Yet I tell you that not even Solomon in all his splendor was dressed like one of these. If that is how God clothes the grass of the field, which is here today and tomorrow is thrown into the fire, will he not much more clothe you, O you of little faith? (Matthew 6:25-30)

Notice that the first thing Jesus says is, "Don't worry about your life." Yet that is exactly what we do. Our days are filled with worries about the very things Jesus said we should not worry about: food, drink, clothing—all the basic necessities of life. Our every waking moment is filled with thoughts and worries about how to get ahead and stay ahead.

In our world today most people approach life in one of two ways: either they work to live or they live to work. Jesus said that both approaches are wrong. He said, "Is not life more important than food, and the body more important than clothes?"

There is more to life than working, even to acquire basic necessities. Work is important, but it does not or should not define us. Our life priority and purpose do not center on work. This is important to know because if we miss our true *priority* in life, we will miss our true *purpose* in life.

Jesus said, "Do not *worry*." Worry is the most useless exercise in the world. Why? Because it doesn't change anything. Most of us spend our time worrying either about things that will never happen or about things that we cannot change. Either way, worrying is pointless. Worry changes nothing, yet it consumes our energy, time, talents, our gifts, our wisdom, and our knowledge. It even consumes our imagination.

The only thing worry contributes is to make us sick. Studies have identified worry-related stress as the number one cause of high blood pressure and cardiovascular disease. Stress causes veins and arteries to constrict, hindering blood flow, causing the blood to back up toward the heart, thus increasing pressure on the heart. This elevates the risk of heart attack and stroke. Worry gets us nowhere. It simply isn't worth our time or trouble.

We worry because we have misplaced priorities, which cause us then to have misplaced faith. Look at the two examples Jesus gave: the birds of the air and the lilies of the field. The birds do not sow or reap or store away food, yet they never go hungry. Likewise, the lilies of the field do not spin fabric and make clothing, yet they are dressed in beauty and elegance that not even King Solomon could match.

Why? Because God Himself feeds the birds and dresses the flowers. Notice that Jesus said of the birds, "your heavenly Father feeds them." He did not say, "*their* heavenly Father." Our heavenly Father is the same one who takes care of the birds of the air and the lilies of the field. The word *Father* (*abba* in Hebrew) means "source and sustainer." So the phrase could read, "your heavenly *Source and Sustainer* feeds them." Jesus' question to us, then, is, "If your heavenly Source and Sustainer takes care of the birds and the lilies, which are here today and gone tomorrow, don't you think He will take care of you, too?"

Our problem today is that we have misplaced our faith. We have changed our source. Instead of looking to our heavenly Father, we look either to ourselves or to someone else (parent, spouse, employer, government) to sustain us. After all, since we live in a dog-eat-dog, every-man-for-himself world, we have to fight, scrape and scramble for everything we can get and then hold onto it with a white-knuckled grip. Right?

That is the priority and mind-set of the world, *not* of the Kingdom of Heaven! Who is your source? If you are looking to anyone other than God the Father and King of Heaven as your source, that may explain why you are struggling and why your life just won't come together. If, on the other hand, you make God your source, then He calls the shots. And if He calls the shots, He pays the bills!

Paganism Is Alive and Well

Any religion that focuses on the acquisition of things and the meeting of personal needs is a religion of pagans. Look again at what Jesus said:

So do not worry, saying, "What shall we eat?" or "What shall we drink?" or "What shall we wear?" For the pagans run after all these things, and your heavenly Father knows that you need them. But seek first His kingdom and His righteousness, and all these things will be given to you as well. Therefore do not worry about tomorrow, for tomorrow will worry about itself. Each day has enough trouble of its own (Matthew 6:31-34).

According to Jesus, always running after and being preoccupied with the acquisition of things and the satisfying of basic necessities is the activity of pagans. Based on that definition, I would have to say that paganism is alive and well in our world today. As a matter of fact, one of the largest gatherings of pagans takes places every Sunday (or Saturday, in the case of Seventh-Day Adventist churches) when the communities known as the church of Jesus Christ gather for worship.

We claim to believe God and trust Him, but our daily lives and the concerns that fill our thoughts reveal that most of us do not. We give lip service to God's provision, yet we work for food, drink, clothing, shelter, and other things as if it all depends on us. And working for those things becomes the center of our existence and the top priority of our lives. We work hard but we don't spend time with God. A couple of hours a week pretending to worship, and that's it. Our preoccupation with material things, satisfying basic needs and getting ahead in the world is nothing other than pagan behavior. Those who truly know the God of Heaven as their Source and Supplier do not have these concerns because they are confident that He has taken care of them.

It is important at this point to understand what we mean by the word *pagan*. Contrary to what many people may assume, most pagans are not atheists; nor are they, usually, evil people. On the contrary, pagans are highly religious. The word *pagan*, in fact, refers to worshipers. It refers to people who worship a god other than the one true and living God as revealed in the Bible. An equivalent word to pagan is *idolater*. Pagans, then, are religious devotees, often highly zealous adherents to a specific system of beliefs and rigidly faithful to a strict set of customs and rituals. The concept of a personal, loving God who cares deeply about them is completely alien to pagans. God, however they conceive him (or her) to be, is a distant, often harsh deity who must be appeased and persuaded to help them. The thought of loving such a god is incomprehensible.

Jesus said that only religious people—pagans—run after the basic needs of life. So if food, drink, clothing, money, car, house and other material things are your priorities, then you are thinking and acting like a pagan, no matter what you claim to believe.

We need a complete change of focus. It is time for us to stop living according to Maslow's hierarchy of needs and start living by the principles and priorities of the Kingdom of Heaven. Jesus turned Maslow upside down and then gave us the correct perspective: *"But seek first His [God's] kingdom and His righteousness, and all these things will be given to you as well"* (Matt. 6:33, emphasis added). They will be given. That means that we do not have to work *for* them or worry *about* them; God will supply them freely if we give priority to His Kingdom and righteousness.

This does not mean that we should quit our jobs and sit around waiting for God to drop all of these things in our laps. It does mean that even as we work from day to day in our jobs and professions, we are living for other priorities—God's priorities—supremely and serenely confident that He has us covered. There is no surer antidote to stress, anxiety, and worry.

It is time to set aside the pagan mind-set with its priority of things and take up instead the divine priority, the priority of the Kingdom of God and His righteousness. Isaiah 26:3 provides this precious promise: *"You will keep him in perfect peace, Whose mind is stayed [steadfast] on You, Because he trusts in You"* (NKJV).

THE PRIORITY OF GOD—KINGDOM FIRST

Our greatest longing is also God's primary intent and desire. God's highest priority is restoring the Kingdom of Heaven on earth. It was to this end that He sent His Son, Jesus Christ, to earth to live among us for a time; to take on human flesh and become one of us. From the very beginning Jesus' message was simple and straightforward: *"Repent, for the kingdom of heaven is near"* (Matt. 4:17b). Later on, He specifically instructed His followers to *"seek first His* [God's] *kingdom and His righteousness, and all these things will be given to you as well"* (Matt. 6:33).

Jesus preached the Kingdom. He taught the Kingdom. The Kingdom of Heaven was the central theme of everything Jesus did and said. It was, essentially, His only message. And that message of the Kingdom is the same message the world needs to hear today because everyone on earth is searching for the Kingdom of Heaven.

The priority of the Kingdom message was brought home to me in a very personal way that transformed my life and my entire way of thinking. Some time ago I had dedicated myself to a private, personal fast. It was a very special time for me because I really wanted to spend some close time with God. My desire was that He would speak to me His heart and mind for that time in my life and reveal His greatest desire for His people. Fifteen days into the fast I sensed God saying to me: *"Kingdom first!"* That was it. Just two words. *Kingdom first!* You might think that after 15 days with no food you would receive at least a sentence from God! But no, He simply said, *"Kingdom first!"* Straight and to the point, which is always the way God speaks.

"Kingdom first!" A deceptively simple statement, so simple that its true depth and significance of meaning are easy to miss. At least, I thought it was simple until I began studying and discovered that this two-word statement embodies the central thrust of God's entire plan and purpose for humankind. For you see, *"Kingdom first!"* is a message with universal application. It relates to everyone on earth. It is a message for the world. *"Kingdom first!"* is a message for Christians, Jews, and Muslims alike. It is for Buddhists and Hindus. It is for atheists and agnostics. It is for scientists, theologians, and philosophers. *"Kingdom first!"* is a message for people of every religion and people of no religion because it is not a religious message. *"Kingdom first!"* is a message that transcends religion.

Why is the *"Kingdom first!"* message so universal and so important? Because when we understand *"Kingdom first!"* we will understand how to live effectively on earth. Everybody wants to live effectively. We all want our lives to mean something. Each of us desires to control our own destiny, live out our dreams, and fulfill our highest potential. Understanding and embracing the *"Kingdom first!"* message will make all of these things possible. It will allow us to understand the keys to life.

PRINCIPLES

1. Nothing is more tragic than a life without purpose.

2. If you're not doing the right thing at the right time, that means you are doing the wrong thing at the wrong time.

3. Priority helps us sharpen our vision so we can focus on the most important things.

4. If you are not pursuing the purpose you were born for, then you are pursuing the wrong thing.

5. Everything man does outside the Kingdom of Heaven is motivated by the drive to meet personal needs.

6. All religion is driven by the priority of needs.

7. Jesus said, "Don't worry about your life."

8. Worry is the most useless exercise in the world.

9. If you make God your source, then He calls the shots. And if He calls the shots, He pays the bills!

10. Any religion that focuses on the acquisition of things and the meeting of personal needs is a religion of pagans.

11. If food, drink, clothing, money, car, house and other material things are your priorities, then you are thinking and acting like a pagan, no matter what you claim to believe.

12. It is time for us to stop living according to Maslow's hierarchy of needs and start living by the principles and priorities of the Kingdom of Heaven.

ENDNOTE

1. Myles Munroe, *Kingdom Principles*, (Shippensburg, PA: Destiny Image Publishers, Inc., 2006), 26.

"You were not created to work for things but to manage things."

CHAPTER THREE

THE EXCLUSIVENESS OF THE DIVINE PRIORITY

When Jesus said, *"Do not worry about your life, what you will eat or drink; or about your body, what you will wear,"* and *"Seek first [God's] kingdom and His righteousness, and all these things will be given to you as well,"* He caused a spiritual earthquake. He turned human culture and society on their ears. With those brief words, Jesus neatly stripped us of everything we think is important. Food, drink, clothing, shelter, cars, money, luxuries; these are the things we live for. These are the things that we get out of bed and go to work for every day. These are the things that make up the objects of most of our prayers. And it is the pursuit of these things that drives human culture and the economies of nations.

Yet, these are the very things Jesus said we should *not* live for. In fact, He told us not even to worry about them. He stripped away all of our confusing, energy-draining, deceptive, distracting, misleading and misplaced priorities and left us with one simple focus: seeking the Kingdom of God. In so doing, He also gave us the key to a simpler, more fulfilling life. Pursuing one central priority in life instead of ten or twenty secondary ones—what could be simpler?

Furthermore, Jesus says that when we make the Kingdom of God our one priority, all these other things that we have spent our lives pursuing will turn around and pursue us! They will chase us down! This is a fundamental principle of the Kingdom of God.

> *Seek first the kingdom of God and His righteousness, and all these things shall be added to you* (Matthew 6:33 NKJV).

This is one of the simplest statements in the Bible, yet one of the least obeyed. We are possessed by our quest for things and for the good life, while God is looking for Kingdom-possessed people. All who seek and gain the Kingdom of God also gain access to all its riches and resources. Why settle for a scrap here and there that we are able to eke out on our own when the fullness of the Kingdom with its abundant provision is available to us?

Kingdom-possessed people do not live just to make a living; they live for the Kingdom. Kingdom-possessed people do not work just to get a paycheck; they work for the Kingdom. Kingdom-possessed people do not strive day in and day out to meet their needs; they strive continually for the Kingdom. As Kingdom citizens and children of God, they know that all these things already belong to them. Kingdom-possessed people understand that their lives are not for the pursuit of selfish gain but for seeking opportunities to introduce others to the Kingdom.

For Kingdom-possessed people, all of life is about the Kingdom of God. To be Kingdom-possessed means to have the Kingdom of God as our sole priority, for the Kingdom priority demands an exclusive claim on our lives. Jesus said, *"No one can serve two masters. Either he will hate the one and love the other, or he will be devoted to the one and despise the other. You cannot serve both God and money"* (Matt. 6:24).

By our Manufacturer's design, we are not equipped to serve two masters. One will always take precedence over the other. There is room in our hearts for one and only one top priority, and Jesus said that top priority must be the Kingdom of God. This is why He said we are to seek *first* God's Kingdom and righteousness.

The Kingdom of God is so vast that our pursuit of it will fill us to capacity so that we have no *room* for other priorities. It also will satisfy us so completely that we have no *need* of other priorities. All the priorities that we recognize as essential or beneficial to life will be satisfied when we set our hearts to seek first the Kingdom of God. This is His promise to us. But He requires our exclusive allegiance. He demands from us our whole heart, our undivided loyalty.

THE PERIL OF DIVIDED LOYALTY

The gospel of the Kingdom of Heaven was the only message Jesus preached, and at every opportunity He reiterated its exclusive nature. The Kingdom priority is exclusive with regard to the cost it exacts from us:

> *As they were walking along the road, a man said to him, "I will follow you wherever you go." Jesus replied, "Foxes have holes and birds of the air have nests, but the Son of Man has no place to lay his head"* (Luke 9:57-58).

How often do we make commitments to God or someone else without first considering what it will cost us in time, energy, money, or inconvenience? We make a promise without realizing what we are getting ourselves into. Later, when we find the requirements to be more than we bargained for, we bail out and end up feeling guilty and defeated because of our failure to follow through.

Like many of us, the man in this passage made a rash promise to follow Jesus wherever He went. No doubt the man was enthusiastic and sincere, but he had not thought through the implications of his promise. Recognizing this, Jesus tested the depth of the man's commitment. He wanted to see how far this man truly was willing to go. Essentially, Jesus said, "The foxes and the birds have homes but I don't. I'm homeless; and if you follow Me you will be homeless too. You will no longer enjoy the creature comforts you are used to. Are you ready for that?"

We are not told how the man responded, but that is not important. What is important to understand is that although seeking first the Kingdom of God results in the most fulfilling and rewarding life possible, that does not mean it is always easy. The cost of seeking the Kingdom is great. What does the King demand from us? Everything. But the rewards are well worth the cost.

As King and Lord of the universe, God owns everything. This means that we own nothing. So it shouldn't be hard for us to let go of things that don't belong to us anyway. And because God owns everything, He can at any time release for our use anything He wishes. But we must first freely give Him everything we have and everything we are.

Many people follow Jesus or "seek" the Kingdom of God for what they hope to get out of it. This is the exact opposite of the correct motivation, according to Jesus. The Kingdom of God is not a "bless me" club. We do not follow God to get Him to pay our bills. We follow Him because He is our King and our heavenly Father. It is in the context of this relationship, and when our priority is right, that He takes care of us and provides for our needs. But seeking the Kingdom comes first. Let me assure you, if you get to the point where you are willing to strip yourself of everything for the sake of God's Kingdom, you are on your way to the greatest life you could ever live!

The Kingdom priority is exclusive also with regard to our relationships, particularly with family:

He said to another man, "Follow me." But the man replied, "Lord, first let me go and bury my father." Jesus said to him, "Let the dead bury their own dead, but you go and proclaim the kingdom of God" (Luke 9:59-60).

Jesus called a man who appeared to be willing to follow Him but the man wanted to wait until after he buried his father. This does not mean necessarily that his father was already dead. The man felt bound by his social, legal, and moral obligation to care for his parents. In Jewish culture, to dishonor one's parents was a gross sin exceeded only by the sin of dishonoring God. Honoring one's parents is so important that God established it as the fifth commandment. Only the commandment to honor God is more important.

Notice how Jesus responded to the man's request. He said, *"Let the dead bury their own dead, but you go and proclaim the kingdom of God."* Jesus was not being dismissive of the fifth commandment or insensitive to the man's sense of duty and responsibility. He was simply saying that no priority takes precedence over the priority of the Kingdom of God. The Kingdom is more important than family, friends, career, or personal ambitions. Nothing is more important than the Kingdom.

To honor God means to obey Him. So to postpone or turn aside from the direct call of God in favor of one's family was to commit a greater sin. God's promise to provide *"all these things"* when we seek first His Kingdom includes caring for the family we may have to leave behind in order to follow God's call. If we take care of the Kingdom, the King will take care of our family.

As Jesus continued down the road, a third man spoke to Him:

> *Still another said, "I will follow you, Lord; but first let me go back and say good-by to my family." Jesus replied, "No one who puts his hand to the plow and looks back is fit for service in the kingdom of God"* (Luke 9:61-62).

Like the second man, this man wanted to follow Jesus, but later, on his own terms, after taking leave of his family. Jesus' response revealed the divided nature of the man's heart. The man wanted to follow Jesus but his whole heart was not in it. He would follow, but would keep looking back to what he left behind. Those who are *"fit for service in the kingdom of God"* have laid aside all other priorities in life except for the Kingdom priority.

These two encounters reveal that the Kingdom priority takes precedence even over the demands and expectations of the family relationship. Both men who spoke to Jesus had the same problem: divided loyalty. They wanted to go with Jesus and they wanted to stay home. Conflicting priorities pulled them in two directions. Their divided loyalty is revealed in how they responded to Jesus. In both cases, they said, "Lord, first…" In the dynamic of the Kingdom of God, those two words never go together; they are incompatible.

The word *lord* means owner or master. We cannot call Christ "Lord," and then say, "But first let me do such and such." If He is Lord, there is no "first"; there is only "yes." Either He owns us or He does not. Either He is our Master or He is not. The Kingdom priority does not allow for divided loyalty. It makes an exclusive claim on our lives.

THE TEST OF KINGDOM PRIORITY

Nowhere in the Bible is the exclusive claim of the Kingdom priority illustrated more clearly than in Jesus' encounter with a wealthy young man of influence and authority. Commonly known as the "rich young ruler," he approached Jesus one day with a very important question:

A certain ruler asked him, "Good teacher, what must I do to inherit eternal life?" "Why do you call Me good?" Jesus answered. "No one is good—except God alone. You know the commandments: 'Do not commit adultery, do not murder, do not steal, do not give false testimony, honor your father and mother.'" "All these I have kept since I was a boy," he said.

When Jesus heard this, He said to him, "You still lack one thing. Sell everything you have and give to the poor, and you will have treasure in Heaven. Then come, follow Me." When he heard this, he became very sad, because he was a man of great wealth (Luke 18:18-23).

By all the common standards of his day, this ruler who approached Jesus was an exemplary young man. He was wealthy (believed generally to be a sign of God's favor), law-abiding and upright in all his behavior; the kind of person that anyone would like to be associated with. He was even religiously devout, careful to observe and obey all the commandments.

Jesus, however, saw what no one else would have noticed. He observed that the man was trying to serve two masters: God and money. This is why He told the man, *"You still lack one thing."* We could do a thousand different things and still miss the most important thing. Success in the wrong assignment is failure. By any worldly measure, this man was successful. Yet he was a failure in Jesus' eyes because he had neglected the most important thing. His heart was divided. He was not a Kingdom-possessed man because his wealth stood in the way. Consequently, Jesus told him, *"Sell everything you have and give to the poor, and you will have treasure in Heaven. Then come, follow Me."* The Kingdom priority claims our all. It demands that we be completely stripped of everything before we start. There is no room in the Kingdom of God for a spirit of ownership.

This was precisely the young man's problem. He believed and assumed that all his wealth belonged to him. Despite his claim to piety and his careful observance of the commandments, money was his true god. His heart was divided between his wealth and his desire to follow God, and when it came down to a choice, he chose his wealth. This is clear from his response to Jesus' demand: *"he became very sad, because he was a man of great wealth."* In the end, he was unwilling to surrender his earthly treasure for treasure in Heaven. He was bound by a spirit of ownership. He failed the test of Kingdom priority.

A spirit of ownership is perhaps the greatest external sign that someone is not in the Kingdom or not yet walking in the priority of Kingdom first. As long as we continue to believe that we own our house, the car in our driveway, the clothes in our closet, the food in our refrigerator, or anything else we "possess," we are not walking in the Kingdom priority. We are not truly seeking first the Kingdom of God. If God cannot ask for and take from us anything He wants anytime He wants without us putting up a fight, then He is not our Lord, no matter what we claim.

THE PERIL OF A SPIRIT OF OWNERSHIP

The rich young ruler went away from Jesus sad because the price of entering the Kingdom of God and gaining treasure in Heaven was more than he was willing to pay. This prompted Jesus to reiterate further to His followers the peril of a spirit of ownership:

> *Jesus looked at him and said, "How hard it is for the rich to enter the kingdom of God! Indeed, it is easier for a camel to go through the eye of a needle than for a rich man to enter the kingdom of God." Those who heard this asked, "Who then can be saved?" Jesus*

replied, "What is impossible with men is possible with God"(Luke 18:24-27).

Wealth, or more specifically, the spirit of ownership, is a hindrance to a person entering the Kingdom of God. The word *enter,* as Jesus used it in this passage, means to "experience the true effect of." In other words, it is hard for a rich man to experience the true effect of what Kingdom living is like because his wealth is his prison. He is so trapped by the pursuit of things that he has no time to pursue the first thing. He has become a prisoner of his own passions.

Jesus then shocked His listeners with His statement that a camel could go through the eye of a needle more easily than a rich man could enter the Kingdom of Heaven. His listeners, entrenched in the belief that wealth was a sign of God's favor, asked, *"Who then can be saved?"* What they were really asking was, "If it is difficult for the rich (the God-favored) to enter the Kingdom of God, then what hope is there for the rest of us?" Jesus assured them that what was impossible in the eyes of men was possible with God.

When Jesus spoke of *"the eye of a needle"* He did not have a sewing needle in mind. In that part of the world, both then and now, the eye of a needle refers also to two wooden posts planted vertically in the ground close enough together so that a camel can squeeze between them only with difficulty. Because of the sand and the dryness of that desert environment, camels can become very dirty very quickly. The eye of a needle is used to help clean dirty camels.

First, the camel driver leads the camel between the two posts until the animal's sides are stuck against them. Thus immobilized, the camel remains still while it receives a bath. Afterward, the driver carefully draws the still-wet camel the rest of the way through the eye of the needle. With this analogy, Jesus was saying that although it is difficult for a rich person to enter the Kingdom of Heaven, it is not impossible. A spirit of ownership can keep us out, but God can help us let go of that spirit.

NOTHING WE GIVE UP FOR THE KINGDOM IS EVER LOST

One reason we should be able to give up the spirit of ownership is because nothing we give up for the Kingdom of God is ever lost. On the contrary, it is multiplied and returned to us. This too is a fundamental principle of the Kingdom of God. Consider this exchange between Peter and Jesus:

> Peter said to him, "We have left all we had to follow you!" "I tell you the truth," Jesus said to them, "no one who has left home or wife or brothers or parents or children for the sake of the kingdom of God will fail to receive many times as much in this age and, in the age to come, eternal life" (Luke 18:28-30).

After the bombshell Jesus dropped about the difficulty of rich people entering the Kingdom of God, Peter may have been feeling a little uncertain about his own status. So he reminded Jesus that he and the rest of Jesus' disciples had left everything in order to follow Him. This may have been Peter's not-so-subtle way of asking, "What's in it for us?"

Jesus' answer reveals that the exclusive nature of the Kingdom priority is not as risky or as outrageous as it may seem at first. In essence, Jesus says that no one who gives up everything for the Kingdom of God has really lost anything, because they will receive *many times as much in this age,* not to mention eternal life in the age to come. Nothing that we give up for the sake of the Kingdom of God do we lose. *Nothing.* The King will return it to us with more besides.

If your priority is to have a nice house, and you live and work day in and day out for that house and the mortgage, and that house is the focus of your life, God may let you have it, but you will miss the fullness of what He wants for you. He says, "If you exchange your priority for Mine—if you give up your priority of a house and take up my priority of the Kingdom—I'll not only give you a house, but I'll give you many houses!"

Whatever we give to the King for the sake of His Kingdom, He will multiply and return to us. The more we give, the more we will receive, not for our own lusts or greedy desires, but so we can seek His Kingdom even more, and help others to do so as well.

Jesus said, *"Seek first His kingdom and His righteousness, and all these things will be given to you as well."* The Kingdom priority is exclusive but it is not limited. God wants you to have *"all these things"*; He just doesn't want them to have you. So forsake everything for the sake of God's Kingdom. Give Him your all and He will give you *"all these things."*

PRINCIPLES

1. God is looking for Kingdom-possessed people.

2. For Kingdom-possessed people, all of life is about the Kingdom of God.

3. The Kingdom priority demands an *exclusive* claim on our lives.

4. The Kingdom priority is exclusive with regard to the cost it exacts from us.

5. The Kingdom of God is not a "bless me" club.

6. The Kingdom priority is exclusive with regard to our relationships, particularly with family.

7. Nothing is more important than the Kingdom.

8. If we take care of the Kingdom, the King will take care of our family.

9. There is no room in the Kingdom of God for a spirit of ownership.

10. Nothing we give up for the Kingdom of God is ever lost. On the contrary, it is multiplied and returned to us.

11. The Kingdom priority is exclusive but it is not limited.

*"Whatever you prioritize
you will pursue."*

CHAPTER FOUR

THE DIVINE
PRIORITY MANDATE

Jesus Christ came to earth to inaugurate a Kingdom, not establish a religion. First, He announced the Kingdom: *"Repent, for the kingdom of Heaven is near"* (Matt. 4:17). Then He taught about the Kingdom wherever He went: *"The kingdom of Heaven is like...."* He identified the Kingdom of God as the first priority of man: *"But seek first His kingdom and His righteousness, and all these things will be given to you as well"* (Matt. 6:33, emphasis added).

Only those who seek the Kingdom of God will find it, and with the seeking comes the understanding of the Kingdom and how it operates. Jesus told His closest followers, *"The knowledge of the secrets of the kingdom of Heaven has been given to you..."* (Matt. 13:11a). When we understand how the Kingdom operates, we will understand how to live in the Kingdom and experience its fullness in our lives.

Our first priority—the principal and most important activity of our life—is to seek the Kingdom of God. But how do we do that? What does it mean to seek God's

Kingdom? How can we find the Kingdom of God if we don't know how to look for it or what to look for? God will never demand from us what He does not supply. He will never instruct us to do something that He doesn't show us how to do.

Even more important, He wants us to seek and find His Kingdom. He gave us this promise: "*You will seek Me and find Me when you seek Me with all your heart*" (Jer. 29:13). Finding God is the same as finding His Kingdom because the two are inseparable. And Jesus assures us: "*Do not be afraid, little flock, for your Father has been pleased to give you the kingdom*" (Luke 12:32).

With these scriptural truths and assurances in mind, let's take a closer look at our divine priority mandate, "*Seek first His kingdom and His righteousness.*" A *mandate* is a command issued by a ruler. Jesus' charge to us to seek first the Kingdom and righteousness of God is a command, not a suggestion. If we claim to be His followers and call Him Lord, we must obey Him. Otherwise, He is not our Lord, we will never find the Kingdom and never experience the fulfillment of our life purpose.

THE DIVINE COMMAND: "SEEK"

The first part of the divine priority is what we can call the divine command: seek. To seek means to pursue with vigor and determination. The idea is that of a diligent, unceasing search until the object of the search is found. In Luke 15 Jesus tells of a man with 100 sheep who lost one, and of a woman with 10 silver coins who lost one, and how both of them searched diligently and did not give up until they recovered that which was lost. This is what it means to seek. We are to pursue the Kingdom of God with determination and vigor.

To seek also means to study. Students seek knowledge and understanding. In the same way, Kingdom citizens must be students of the Kingdom and of its constitution, the Bible. Psalm 1:2 says that the blessed man delights in the law of the Lord and meditates on it day and night. Paul, New Testament ambassador of the King, counsels us to, *"Be diligent to present yourself approved to God, a worker who does not need to be ashamed, rightly dividing the word of truth"* (2 Tim. 2:15 NKJV). The Greek word for "be diligent" is *spoudazo*, which also means "study" or "labor." Seeking the Kingdom means studying it with diligence. Only by committed and rigorous study can the secrets of the Kingdom and the Word of God become known to us. As we study, the Spirit of God will open our minds to understand.

Seeking also means to explore. Human explorers through the ages traveled the globe seeking new lands, new peoples, new horizons. Exploring carries the element of high adventure, and the Kingdom of God is indeed an adventure. We must explore the Kingdom; we must explore its power, its laws, its government, its culture, its society, its commands, its economy, its taxation—everything. The Kingdom of God is so vast that we could spend the rest of our lives exploring it yet only scratch the surface.

Another critical aspect of seeking is understanding. We could pursue something, seeking it diligently, yet not understand it when we found it. Without understanding, the search is not complete. Nothing is truly ours until we understand it. Until we understand the Kingdom we cannot properly teach it, pass it on or fully realize its benefits and blessings. Once we understand for ourselves, then the promises of the Kingdom will begin manifesting in our lives.

Closely related to study and understanding, to seek also means to learn. Learning is more than mental knowledge of facts and information; the knowledge must be reproducible in practical terms. This means demonstrating the ability to perform the action learned as well as teach it to someone else so that they learn it also.

Seeking often involves taking the time to consider, to sit and ponder something in an effort to understand. This is similar, of course, to meditation. Some things require deep thought and analysis before they become comprehensible. The psalmist said, "*When I consider your heavens, the work of your fingers, the moon and stars, which you have set in place, what is man that you are mindful of him, and the son of man that you care for him?*" (Ps. 8:3-4)

Jesus said, "*Why do you worry about clothing? Consider the lilies of the field, how they grow: they neither toil nor spin, and yet I say to you that even Solomon in all his glory was not arrayed like one of these*" (Matt. 6:28-29 NKJV). We need to take the Word of God and consider it, ponder it, chew on it, memorize it, and the more we do so the more we will comprehend.

When we seek something, we have a desire to know. Who pursues something he has no interest in? Who takes the time to ponder something that means nothing to him? If we desire to know the Kingdom and its ways, the King will make sure our desire is satisfied. Jesus said, *"Blessed are those who hunger and thirst for righteousness, for they will be filled"* (Matt. 5:6).

Not only should we desire the Kingdom, we should have a passion for the Kingdom! What are you passionate about? What gets your blood going in the morning? What infuses your life with purpose? Everyone is passionate about something. If you are not passionate about the Kingdom of God, then you are focused on the wrong thing.

Anything worth seeking is worth pursuing with diligent dedication. Diligence always involves discipline. If we want to seek the Kingdom it may mean disciplining ourselves to turn off the TV so we can study the Word of God. It may mean rearranging our schedule in order to have more time to pray. It may mean reordering our time priorities to ensure we get enough sleep so that we're not "too tired" to gather with other believers for worship. Seeking the Kingdom is deliberate and proactive. We will never stumble on it by accident. We must plan for it.

Finally, to seek the Kingdom means to become preoccupied with the Kingdom. If we are seeking the Kingdom, that means we are thinking about it all day long. It possesses us. Everywhere we go and with everything we do and say we are focused on the Kingdom. We evaluate every decision in light of how it will affect our pursuit of the Kingdom. Our every thought, word, motive, and action is "Kingdom First!"

THE DIVINE PRIORITY: "FIRST"

If the Divine Command is to seek the Kingdom of God, the Divine Priority is that we must seek it *first.* Seeking the Kingdom first means that we pursue it as the *principal thing,* the first thing above and before and beyond all other things. First means that the Kingdom of God is more important to us than anything else. It means that we place the highest value of all on the Kingdom and stand ready to sacrifice anything and everything else for its sake. First means that we establish the Kingdom as our primary interest. All other priorities in life are secondary to the priority of the Kingdom and so far below it as to be almost nonexistent by comparison.

Kingdom first does not mean first among many but first and only. When God told the Israelites, "*You shall have no other gods before Me*" (Exod. 20:3), He was not saying, "As long as you worship Me first and foremost, you can have other gods." What He meant was that they were never to bring any other gods before His face or into His presence. God claimed exclusive rights to their worship, love, and devotion. The "Kingdom First!" priority is just as exclusive.

Seeking the Kingdom of God first means considering the interests of the Kingdom before making decisions—when and where we go to school, who we marry, what job we accept, how we spend our money. Before deciding on these and other issues, we need to ask the question, "Is this in line with the Kingdom of God?" Every day we are bombarded with opportunities to compromise our morality, honesty, integrity, and character. Your boss asks you to do something dishonest at work. Your boyfriend or girlfriend tries to talk you into an immoral relationship. You are tempted to cheat on your taxes.

Learn to ask yourself, "Will this be pleasing to the Kingdom?" It's not worth violating the principles of the Kingdom for the sake of expediency or to avoid offending someone or rocking the boat. Developing the habit of considering the Kingdom first will help you avoid a lot of mistakes and bad decisions.

THE DIVINE OBJECT: "THE KINGDOM OF GOD"

It is one thing to know how to seek the Kingdom of God but quite another to understand that Kingdom and the principles under which it operates. For detailed information on this subject, I refer you to the two earlier books in this series: *Rediscovering the Kingdom*[1] and *Kingdom Principles*.[2]

Few people in the world today live in a true kingdom, particularly in the West, so almost no one knows what kingdom life is really like. Consequently, Kingdom language in the Bible often can seem confusing or alien to modern readers. If the Kingdom priority is so important, we had better know what the Kingdom is and how it functions.

So what is the Kingdom? Simply stated, the Kingdom is God's government. It is His rulership and dominion over Heaven and earth. In practical terms it refers to His universal jurisdiction and executed will over all creation.

I can still remember what life was like in a kingdom. When I was born, my nation, the Bahamas, was still under the jurisdiction of the British crown. We were a colony of Great Britain. The British monarch's dominion included the islands of the Bahamas. This is why our entire nation was called "Crown land." All the land belonged to the reigning king or queen because in a true kingdom, the king owns both the land and the people. So when Jesus said we are to seek first the Kingdom of God, He was telling us to seek first the ownership of God over ourselves and everything we have in life.

The word *kingdom* also means to have influence over a territory. When we seek first the Kingdom of God we are seeking His influence to be extended over the entire world in our private life, our business life, our marriage life, our relationships, our sexual life, and all other dimensions of life.

Part of this influence has to do with administration. In the Kingdom of God we are under the administration of Heaven. This means that God, the King, becomes our reference point for everything. His will becomes our will, His ways become our ways, His culture becomes our culture, His society becomes our society, and His interests become our interests. As Kingdom citizens and children of the King through Christ, we become ambassadors on earth of His heavenly Kingdom.

Influence also means impact. Kings and queens impact the land and the lives of the people over whom they rule. This is certainly true in the Bahamas. Although we are today an independent nation, we still reflect in many ways the lingering British influence from our colonial days. For one thing, we drive on the left side of the street, just as in England. In contrast, our friends in the United States, a nation that forcibly withdrew from under British dominion, drive on the right side. Yet even to this day the United States continues to reflect in many ways the heritage of its British colonial past.

Americans, by the way they live, prove that they are not under a political earthly kingdom. The islands of the Bahamas were under British rule far longer than were the American colonies. Consequently, Britain's impact on Bahamian life, law, and culture has been more substantial and more enduring. And that influence is reflected in our daily lives.

This raises an important point: *we can tell which kingdom we are in by the way we live.* If we claim to believe and follow the King, our lives will reflect the influence of His government and administration. Other people who are not in the Kingdom will wonder, and perhaps even ask, why we are so different. It is because we are under a different administration from that of the world; a different government, a different culture, and a different law.

Jesus said, *"By their fruit you will recognize them. Do people pick grapes from thornbushes, or figs from thistles? Likewise every good tree bears good fruit, but a bad tree bears bad fruit. A good tree cannot bear bad fruit, and a bad tree cannot bear good fruit"* (Matt. 7:16-18). This means that others can tell what kind of tree we are by what we produce in our lives. Our lives are supposed to manifest the fruit—the influence—of the Kingdom of God so that anybody can look at us and tell where our allegiance lies.

In the Bible, the Hebrew word for "kingdom" is *mamlakah*; the New Testament Greek word is *basileia*. Both words carry the same general range of meaning: king, sovereignty, dominion, control, reign, rulership, and royal power. Considering all of these terms and characteristics, we can define a kingdom, then, as:

> The governing influence of a king over his territory (domain), impacting it with his personal will, purpose and intent, producing a culture, values, morals and lifestyle that reflect the king's desire and nature for his citizens.

This describes perfectly the Kingdom of God, which is the Kingdom that Jesus commanded us to "seek first." And it is in the seeking of this Kingdom—not in religion— that we will receive from the King "all these things," all the daily needs of life that the rest of the world toils and labors and frets and worries and strives and scrambles for. No religion has such a guarantee as the Kingdom guarantee.

The Divine Position: God's Righteousness

In addition to seeking first the Kingdom of God, we are to seek also His righteousness. This is not a first and second priority but two parts of one complete whole. God's Kingdom cannot be separated from His righteousness. A kingdom always reflects the nature and character of the king. God is righteous and therefore His Kingdom is also righteous.

Only righteous people will enter the Kingdom. The problem is that none of us are righteous on our own. As David, psalmist and king of Israel wrote, *"The Lord looks down from Heaven on the sons of men to see if there are any who understand, any who seek God. All have turned aside, they have together become corrupt; there is no one who does good, not even one"* (Ps. 14:2-3). When we are born again through the new birth by repentance of sin and faith in Christ, God imputes righteousness to us. He declares us righteous on the basis of the righteousness of His Son and we gain entrance into the Kingdom.

The New Testament calls this transaction *justification*. Justification is a legal term, not a religious term. It means to declare someone innocent just as if that person had never committed an offense. When we are justified in Christ, we receive a royal pardon from the King. He naturalizes us as citizens of His Kingdom and all the rights, privileges, and resources of the Kingdom become ours. But we also come under the government and administration of the Kingdom and are accountable to the King.

Seeking the righteousness of God is extremely important because His righteousness protects us. It keeps us under the Kingdom covering. And once we are under the Kingdom covering, all the additions—"all these things"—become automatic.

Like justification, the word *righteous* is a legal term. It means "right positioning, to be in correct alignment with the ruling standard." To be righteous means that we do not violate the laws of the government. A righteous person is in right standing with authority. Right standing carries with it the even deeper element of being in fellowship with that authority. As long as we abide by the laws and standards of government, we have nothing to fear. Our conscience is clear. The moment we break the law, however, our fellowship and right standing with the ruling authority is broken. We are no longer righteous.

As an example, imagine driving down the road in your car. As long as you observe the speed limit and make no moving violations, you have nothing to worry about. Penalty and punishment are the farthest things from your mind. Suppose, however, that you accidentally travel through a red light. Now what happens? Immediately you check your mirrors to see if the police are coming after you. You broke the law. You're guilty and you know it and you hope no one saw you. But your guilt creates tension in your mind because you know you are now out of alignment with the ruling standard.

This analogy perfectly describes the dilemma faced by the human race. None of us are righteous. We are all out of alignment with the ruling standard, with God's standard. Why? Because when Adam sinned, his sinfulness passed to every succeeding generation, corrupting the entire race of man. Sin is rebellion against God's Kingly authority. If we want to enter the Kingdom of God, our right standing with God must be restored. This is why Jesus Christ came to earth, not only to announce the coming of the Kingdom but also so that through His sinless death we could be made righteous in Him. Jesus came and died so we could enter the Kingdom.

If you want to be righteous, you've got to submit, not to religion, but to Jesus Christ, the King who gave His blood for you. His blood cleanses the stain of rebellion and removes your guilt. He puts you back in right standing with Himself. You start driving on His side of the street. You start eating what He eats and drinking what He drinks. You begin conforming your life to His in every way possible because you are under His Kingdom. You are righteous.

God has committed Himself to you because you now are in right relationship with Him. To be righteous means that you are legal, lawful, in sync with the government. Nothing stands between you and the law. Therefore, you need not fear authority. If you keep the laws of God, He will protect you. Stay in the law and everything you need will come to you. The Bible says that even the wealth of the wicked is laid up for the righteous (see Prov. 13:22). And who are the righteous? Those who are within the law.

PRINCIPLES

1. Our first priority—the principal and most important activity of our life—is to seek the Kingdom of God.

2. If we desire to know the Kingdom and its ways, the King will make sure our desire is satisfied.

3. Seeking the Kingdom is deliberate and proactive.

4. Kingdom first does not mean first among many, but first and only.

5. When Jesus said we are to seek first the Kingdom of God, He was telling us to seek first the ownership of God over ourselves and everything we have in life.

6. We can tell which kingdom we are in by the way we live.

7. Only righteous people will enter the Kingdom.

8. When we are justified in Christ, we receive a royal pardon from the King.

9. The word *righteous* means "right positioning, to be in correct alignment with the ruling standard."

10. None of us are righteous.

11. Jesus came and died so we could enter the Kingdom.

ENDNOTES

1. Myles Munroe, *Rediscovering the Kingdom: Ancient Hope for Our 21st Century World,* (Shippensburg, PA: Destiny Image Publishers, Inc., in partnership with Diplomat Press, Nassau, Bahamas, 2004.)

2. Myles Munroe, *Kingdom Principles: Preparing for Kingdom Experience and Expansion,* (Shippensburg, PA: Destiny Image Publishers, Inc., in partnership with Diplomat Press, Nassau, Bahamas, 2006.)

*"Correct alignment with truth
principles guarantees success in life."*

CHAPTER FIVE

THE POWER
OF RIGHTEOUSNESS

One of humankind's greatest struggles is determining what is most important in life. Each of us must at some point decide what we are living for if our lives are to have focus and a sense of purpose. Compounding the challenge is the fact that we live in a culture that regards truth as relative and life as meaningless. If life is an evolutionary accident, then there is no such thing as absolute truth or morality and no high and exalted purpose for human existence. Consequently, many people give up on life and, if they don't commit suicide first, retreat into a mind-set of cynicism, hopelessness, and despair.

At the same time, there are many people who yearn for a simpler life free of the stress, struggles, and hectic pace of our high-speed, high-tech, multiple-option, anything-goes society. With so many choices, how do you choose the best, the most important? How do you make sure that you are spending your life on the things that really count?

Over the last 30 years or so my life has become very simple. That does not mean I am not busy. My life is quite full. I frequently travel internationally and rarely have an empty schedule. Yet, in spite of my "busyness," my life is simple because I have spent the last three decades learning to live according God's priorities. The world offers a "grab bag" of possibilities to choose from, but as mentioned previously, Jesus reduces the issues of life to two things: the Kingdom of God and the righteousness of God. That's it. Everything else in life is a byproduct.

When I first understood this as teenager, it changed my life. It is amazing how simple life becomes when you realize that you need to focus only on two things. Even a busy life can be simple when it has been stripped of everything distracting and counterproductive to the pursuit of God's Kingdom and righteousness.

As we have already seen, the command to seek first the Kingdom and righteousness of God comes with a corollary promise that "all these things" the world strives for will be given, or added, to us. Think about this: anything you work for was not added. Added means you receive something you did not work for. God blesses most of us with the health and ability to work for the things we need to support ourselves and our families but, as I've said before, we should never *live* for those things. If our priority is focused on the Kingdom and righteousness of God, He will add all the rest to us. He wants to give us many things that we did not and even cannot work for. But the key to this life of favor and blessing is to seek, to pursue, to walk in the righteousness of God.

DEFINING RIGHTEOUSNESS

God's Kingdom and God's righteousness. Both are equally important and, as you read earlier, both are inseparable. A kingdom always reflects the nature of its king. Righteousness begets righteousness and unrighteousness begets unrighteousness. Righteousness is the nature and defining characteristic of the Kingdom of God. As I mentioned briefly in Chapter Four, the Hebrew word for kingdom, *mamlakah,* means "dominion and royal government." We are to seek first the *mamlakah* of God. This takes in many things: God's government, rulership, and dominion over the earth, His jurisdiction and executed will, the influence of Heaven on earth, God's administration, and His impact on the earth. So the first thing we are supposed to do—the first issue of our lives—is to get under God's government.

Let me put it another way: seek God's *citizenship.* Joining a religion won't solve your problems. Neither will joining a fraternity or a lodge. The only way to solve our greatest problems and satisfy our greatest needs is to place ourselves under the Kingdom on earth.

With the Kingdom of God comes His righteousness. We cannot inhabit His Kingdom without it. What does it mean to be righteous? I touched on it a little in the last chapter but now it is time to dig deeper. Righteousness, or the lack of it, affects our whole life. It is too important a principle to pass over lightly.

The basic New Testament Greek word for "righteous" is *dikaios,* a powerful word that means "those who are upright, just, righteous, conforming to God's laws." It also carries the quality of being without prejudice or partiality. A related word, *dikaiosune,* means "righteousness" or "uprightness." In the Old Testament, two related Hebrew words, *sedeq* and *sedaqah,* carry the meaning, righteousness. They are relational words, just as righteousness has to do with man's relationship to God. *Sedeq* and *sedaqah* are legal terms signifying justice in conformity with the legal corpus (the Law; see Deut. 16:20), the judicial process (see Jer. 22:3), the justice of the king as judge (see 1 Kings 10:9; Ps. 119:121; Prov. 8:15), and also the source of justice, God Himself.[1] *Legal corpus* means the body of law that runs a country.

Heaven is a country; an invisible country, but a country nonetheless. The government of Heaven is under the authority of the King of Glory, the Lord of Hosts, the God of the universe who created the earth and put humankind here as His vice-regents. We were created to be local kings ruling under the jurisdiction of the universal King.

As I said before, righteousness is a legal word, not a religious word. It has to do with citizens' relationship with their government, and that relationship is based on the citizens obeying the laws of the country so they do not come into conflict with government authority and jeopardize their citizenship privileges. Every country demands righteousness, whether it is a republic, a democracy, a communist state, or a kingdom, because righteousness simply means to be in conformity with the laws of the country.

In the Bible, the word *righteousness* almost always is linked in close proximity to the word *justice,* which means "rights." Righteousness is always related to justice because righteousness is a prerequisite for justice. Every country operates under a written constitution of some kind. A constitution is a contract with the people that lays out the laws and rights that will govern the nation. It spells out what the government expects from the citizens and what the citizens can expect from the government. Furthermore, it specifies the penalties for violating the law as well as the legal recourses available for those whose rights have been violated to receive justice.

Like the nations of the earth, the Kingdom of God also has a constitution—the Bible. Unlike many earthly nations where the people write the constitution, in the Kingdom of God the King Himself wrote the constitution. In a kingdom, the king's word is law. The citizens cannot debate it, challenge it, or change it. So in relation to the Kingdom of God, all of us stand either in alignment or out of alignment with Kingdom law, the Word of God. We are either righteous or unrighteous. It is a matter of positioning.

Righteousness means right positioning with the government. It is when a person takes up citizenship in a country and pledges to obey its laws. Those are simple requirements. When Jesus said, "*Seek first the Kingdom of*

God and His righteousness," He was saying, "Seek to become a citizen of the Kingdom of God and then stay in alignment with the government's law. If you do those two things—citizenship and obedience to the laws—then everything you need will be added to you." What could be simpler?

TWO PRIORITIES FOR MAN

So, there are two priorities for us: Kingdom and righteousness. Kingdom is the horizontal dimension that deals with *power*: rulership, dominion and control. It is kingship. Righteousness, on the other hand, is the vertical dimension that deals with *position*: relationship, right standing, disposition, and authority. It is priesthood. There is no dichotomy in the mind of God between priest and king.

Righteous citizens are law-abiding citizens. Citizen relates to kingship; it is the power part. Law-abiding relates to priesthood; it is the positioning part. As citizens of the Kingdom of God, we are both kings and priests: *"To Him who loved us...and has made us kings and priests to His God and Father..."* (Rev. 1:5b-6 NKJV); *"But you are a chosen people, a royal priesthood, a holy nation, a people belonging to God..."* (1 Pet. 2:9a). There are no schizophrenics in the Kingdom of God. We are all kings and priests together.

Righteousness is our relationship with the government. Kingdom is our disposition with the government. It is our right to rule. So, Kingdom is rulership. Kingdom is dominion. Righteousness is our right standing within that dominion. The purpose of a priest is to keep people related to God. As Kingdom citizens we are each our own priest. We are supposed to "work out" our own salvation (Phil. 2:12). We are supposed to protect our own selves by not disobeying the law.

Let me put it another way. Returning to our driving analogy from the last chapter, every time you stop at a red light you are a priest. As long as you stop at the red light, you have the right for no police officer to arrest you. By choosing to obey the law, you are acting as your own priest, maintaining your right alignment with the government.

Priesthood is the vertical dimension and kingship is the horizontal dimension. If you keep the vertical clear, the horizontal will be clear. As long as you are an effective priest, you will be an effective king. Righteousness, therefore, is the key. For this reason, righteousness is more important than kingship. Kingdom makes you a citizen, but righteousness gives you access to all the rights, resources and privileges of citizenship. Get yourself out of alignment with the government and those rights and privileges can be suspended, just as they are for citizens of a nation who are in prison for crimes they committed. They are still citizens but they no longer enjoy the full rights and freedoms of citizens who are not incarcerated.

This explains why many born-again Kingdom citizens struggle with basic needs from day to day and do not experience the fullness of Kingdom living. They are not taking proper care to stay in right standing with their government. By violating the laws and principles of the Kingdom, they cut themselves off from access to its resources. Righteousness, then, is the key to abundant Kingdom living.

The key to success in a kingdom is for the citizens to maintain right relationship with the government. This is righteousness. At the same time, the government is responsible for the rights and well-being of the citizens. Citizens benefit from their righteous relationship by qualifying to make demands on the government. Righteousness gives you power. If you are keeping the law, then all the rights of the constitution are yours. Citizens have rights. Righteous citizens can demand what is rightfully theirs. That is why it is a legal term.

Our two priorities are to seek Kingdom citizenship and the relationship that puts us in a position to demand things from the Kingdom. And the Kingdom government is responsible and obligated to the citizen. Righteousness gives us rights and rights activate the government to act on our behalf.

To clarify further, let's summarize the relationship between Kingdom and righteousness this way:

- The kingdom places us in citizenship; righteousness places in us relationship.

- Kingdom gives us rights to government benefits; righteousness gives us access to government benefits.

- Kingdom makes us legal; righteousness maintains our legal status.

- Righteousness is manifested in holiness.

Holiness is not a doctrine; it is a result. Jesus never taught on holiness. He taught on the Kingdom and righteousness. Living holy simply means you are obeying all the Kingdom laws. If you are righteous, you don't have to "do" holiness; it is a by-product of right standing. Holiness is a manifestation of righteousness. Food, clothing, and rituals don't make you holy. Holiness is based on relationship, and relationship comes from righteousness.

POWER KEYS TO KINGDOM LIFE

Where does the power in righteousness come from? It comes from the King, who passes it down to us. The New Testament Book of Hebrews attests to this:

But about the Son he says, "Your throne, Oh God, will last forever and ever, and righteousness will be the scepter of your kingdom. You have loved righteousness and hated wickedness; therefore God, your God, has set you above your companions by anointing you with the oil of joy" (Hebrews 1:8-9).

A scepter is the symbol of a king's royal authority. If the king extends the scepter to you, it means you may enter his presence for an audience. If he does not, you must remain outside. In ancient times this was a matter of life or death. The Book of Esther describes how the king of Persia would extend his scepter for those he granted permission to enter. Anyone who entered the king's presence without the extended scepter was killed on the spot. Even Queen Esther risked death if she entered the king's presence without his scepter extended to her.

The scepter was a visible symbol of the king's power. When the King extends His scepter to us, we may enter and everything in the Kingdom becomes ours. The passage says, *"righteousness will be the scepter of your kingdom."* This means that our authority in the Kingdom of God is righteousness. As long as we stay lined up with the government's laws, we have power with the government. God gives us power to ask for anything we need. He hands it to us.

Righteousness is also the standard by which the King dispenses judgment:

> *He will judge the world in righteousness; He will govern the peoples with justice* (Psalm 9:8).

God will judge the world as to whether the governments of the earth are lined up with Heaven.

> *And the heavens proclaim His righteousness, for God Himself is judge* (Psalm 50:6)

If we remain lined up, God gives us our rights.

> *Righteousness and justice are the foundation of Your throne; love and faithfulness go before You* (Psalm 89:14).

The foundation for our exercising the authority of God is our relationship with God. Once we are lined up with God, He will lavish His faithfulness and love upon us. Talk about getting your needs met! God says, "Get into right position with me, and I'll overload you."

Here are seven more power keys. The power of righteousness is:

1. Governmental obligation. When you are in right standing with the King, He is obligated to take care of your life.

2. Governmental protection. When you are in right standing with the King, He is obligated to protect you.

3. Governmental support. When you are in right standing with the King, He is obligated to support your life, to uphold you in everything.

4. Governmental provisions. When you are in right standing with the King, He provides you with everything you need.

5. Governmental commitment. When you are in right standing with the King, the King is committed to take care of you.

6. Governmental responsibility. When you are under a King's authority and are in right relationship with that King, the King has a place of responsibility toward you.

7. Righteousness activates the government. When you are in right standing with the King, you activate the entire machine of the government. The government is focused upon you. It does everything for you. *"For the eyes of the Lord range throughout the earth to strengthen those whose hearts are fully committed to Him..."* (2 Chron. 16:9). God's eyes are on the righteous. Our righteousness activates the government. His own nature and promises obligate Him to act.

What a powerful list!

CONSTITUTIONAL PRINCIPLES FOR THE PURSUIT OF RIGHTEOUSNESS

If you want to know how an appliance works, you turn to the owners' manual prepared by the manufacturer. If you want to understand the principles under which a nation or a kingdom operates, you examine its constitution. The pursuit of righteousness is the fundamental operating principle for citizens of the Kingdom of God. There is no better way to learn how to conduct that pursuit than by consulting and following the Kingdom constitution, the Bible. Let's examine some of the constitutional principles that help us understand, apply, and exercise righteousness.

Wealth is worthless in the day of wrath, but righteousness delivers from death (Proverbs 11:4).

Do you want long life? Then live for righteousness. Don't live for wealth. The pursuit of righteousness may bring wealth your way, but as a by-product. Righteousness is its own reward. Living for righteousness will deliver you from the death of your business, the death of your marriage, the death of your investments, the death of your finances, the death of your health. If you are lined up with God, He will deliver you.

> *The righteousness of the blameless makes a straight way for them, but the wicked are brought down by their own wickedness* (Proverbs 11:5).

Blameless means clean living that is above reproach. You stop for red lights. You are honest in all your dealings, even when no one would know if you weren't. You seek to obey God every minute of every day. Righteousness will clear the path ahead of you so that nothing stands between you and full, abundant living. If righteousness is its own reward, then wickedness is its own curse. The wicked may seem to prosper for a time, but eventually their own wickedness will destroy them.

> *The righteousness of the upright delivers them, but the unfaithful are trapped by evil desires* (Proverbs 11:6).

Righteousness is true freedom; freedom to live as God meant for you to live: happy, healthy, abundant, prosperous, and master of your circumstances. Unrighteousness is bondage that will shackle you to your baser lusts and desires.

In the way of righteousness there is life; along that path is immortality (Proverbs 12:28).

When you are lined up with God, you cannot die! Righteousness makes you immortal to enjoy the Kingdom and its benefits forever! How's that for destiny?!

Righteousness guards the man of integrity, but wickedness overthrows the sinner (Proverbs 13:6).

Alignment with God and His Word places you under His protection. Living with integrity will build you a good reputation that will hold you in good stead when you come under attack from the unscrupulous. A wicked man, however, eventually will be undone by his own wickedness.

Better is little with righteousness than much gain with injustice (Proverbs 16:8).

I'd rather be right with God than be right with the world. In fact, James 4:4 states that to be a friend of the world is to be an enemy of God. The world as a whole opposes God and everything He stands for. That is why the world needs to be told about the Kingdom. Be satisfied and faithful with the little you may have now because, if you are righteous, God will add more that you did not have to work or scheme or connive for. Unjust gain is a dead end.

Righteousness exalts a nation, but sin is a disgrace to any people (Proverbs 14:34).

Righteousness is not only personal but also corporate. Personal righteousness can exist without corporate righteousness, but there is no corporate righteousness without personal righteousness. It takes righteous people to create a righteous nation, and diligence on their part to keep the nation righteous. Every law enacted and every bill passed should be measured against and brought into alignment with the standard of God's Word. Otherwise, unrighteousness will result. We see this happening all over the world, particularly in the historically "Christian" West. Every misaligned law or other action at the national level leads the nation farther down the path of disgrace, dissension, disillusionment, disintegration and, eventually, dissolution. None of us as Kingdom citizens can afford to be satisfied merely with our own private righteousness. We must be alert, vigilant, engaged and even militant in pressing for righteousness at the corporate and national levels. Otherwise we risk bringing the judgment of God down on our nations.

The Lord detests the way of the wicked but He loves those who pursue righteousness (Proverbs 15:9).

Notice that the Lord detests the way of the wicked. God loves wicked people, but He hates their wicked ways. He wants to change their hearts so they will pursue righteousness instead of wickedness. Remember, all of us once were wicked in God's sight until we were transformed through the blood of Christ, brought into right standing with God, and made citizens of His Kingdom. Not only does God love the righteous, He loves those

who want to do right. He will move Heaven and earth to
help an honest seeker of righteousness find it.

> *The Lord has dealt with me according to my righ-
> teousness; according to the cleanness of my hands He
> has rewarded me. For I have kept the ways of the
> Lord; I have not done evil by turning from my God.
> All his laws are before me; I have not turned away
> from His decrees. I have been blameless before Him
> and have kept myself from sin. The Lord has
> rewarded me according to my righteousness, accord-
> ing to the cleanness of my hands in His sight* (Psalm
> 18:20-24).

This is without doubt one of the finest descriptions
in the Bible of practical righteousness—righteousness as
it is lived out from day to day. David, future king of
Israel, describes the righteous life as a life of obedience to
the Word and ways of God. Righteousness brings reward
and the link between the two is obedience. Reward is that
which is added. It is not something we work for. If we are
righteous, "all these things" will be added to us. We will
receive our reward, both in this life and in the life to
come.

> *The Lord is my shepherd, I shall not be in want. He
> makes me lie down in green pastures, He leads me
> beside quiet waters, He restores my soul. He leads me
> in paths of righteousness for His name's sake* (Psalm
> 23:1-3).

Why does the Lord take care of us? Why does He
give us green pastures and quiet waters? Why does He

restore our soul and lead us in paths of righteousness? For the sake of His name. For the sake of His reputation. He is saying to us, "Do right, please, so I can protect My Name. Do right, so I can take care of you and show Myself to be a good and benevolent King. Don't call me 'Lord' and then not do what I say. Let me show the world how a Kingdom citizen lives: in peace, prosperity, abundance, and security."

> *Vindicate me in your righteousness, O Lord my God;*
> *do not let them gloat over me* (Psalm 35:24).

The word *vindicate* means "to deliver or avenge, to justify or defend, to free from allegation or blame." Righteousness sets us up for the Lord to defend us from unjustified accusation and attack. No matter what you may be going through on your job or elsewhere, no matter what pressure you may be under to compromise your integrity, honor, or principles, just stay aligned with God and He will come to your defense. You may feel as though everybody is conspiring against you. Don't worry about it. Even if you are the only righteous person there, God can vindicate you. Whatever you are going through, God says, "I will give the answer. I'm going to do this Myself. You just remain righteous. Stay lined up with My government."

> *He who pursues righteousness and love finds life,*
> *prosperity and honor* (Proverbs 21:21).

The world pursues prosperity and the good life but rarely finds them. Kingdom citizens, however, are to pursue righteousness. We are never to pursue prosperity. There is no "prosperity gospel" in the Kingdom.

Prosperity is a by-product of righteous living. Live righteously and what happens? You will find prosperity. You will find the good life and the abundant life. You will find honor in the eyes of God and men. You won't have to pursue them to procure them. All these things you will find simply by putting all your energy into one thing: the pursuit of righteousness.

> *Of the increase of His government and peace there will be no end. He will reign on David's throne and over His kingdom, establishing and upholding it with justice and righteousness from that time on and forever. The zeal of the Lord Almighty will accomplish this* (Isaiah 9:7).

This verse refers to Jesus Christ, who came to restore man back to his relationship with the Kingdom of God. His is the Kingdom that will last forever and be characterized by justice and righteousness. A just and righteous King will always give His citizens their rights based upon their being and remaining aligned to the principles and laws of His Kingdom.

> *...with righteousness He will judge the needy, with justice He will give decisions for the poor of the earth...*(Isaiah 11:4).

This verse says that poverty is solved by righteousness. If a poor man becomes righteous—lined up with the Kingdom—his poverty is gone. To judge means to give rights. In other words, poverty is really a result of disposition.

I was born in the low part of my country. My only reason for coming out of whatever I was in is my relationship with God. Nothing else explains it. Righteousness is the solution to poverty. This means that unrighteousness is the cause of poverty. Let me hasten to add, however, that often it is the unrighteousness of those who oppress and take advantage of the poor that helps perpetuate poverty. Unrighteousness affects not only us but also all those who are within our sphere of influence. Even under oppressive conditions, however, the transformed mind-set of a Kingdom citizen who is poor can manifest in changed external circumstances. The King takes care of His righteous citizens no matter where they are or what their condition.

A king will reign in righteousness and rulers will rule with justice (Isaiah 32:1).

Every leader, political or otherwise, should take this verse to heart. Alignment with Heaven's government is the key to the success of any country. For a king to reign in righteousness he must be lined up with the government of Heaven. This is how any nation prospers. All judges should judge everything according to the Word of God. All of our morals, policies and values should conform to God's laws. Otherwise, the nation will be unrighteous and on the road to disaster.

In every nation today there is a crying need for righteous Kingdom citizens to be active in the political arena, not only as voters but also as candidates and office holders. The only way for justice to prevail for every citizen of a nation is for that nation to be governed by principles of righteousness laid out in the Word of God. And the only way for righteousness to govern a nation is for righteous citizens to wield their influence and example at every level of government.

The fruit of righteousness will be peace; the effect of righteousness will be quietness and confidence forever (Isaiah 32:17).

There it is. When you are righteous, you fly your flag. When you are righteous you keep the company you work for afloat. When you are righteous, you keep the home at peace. When you are righteous, you bring peace to a company because you work there.

This is why the Bible says that as long as Joseph was with Pharaoh, Egypt prospered. When Daniel was with Nebuchadnezzar, the country prospered. Because you are in that school, the school is blessed. Don't ever make light of your influence on where you are because righteousness brings peace.

Peace, quietness, confidence. Don't you love those words? Don't you wish they were the norm for your life? Quietness means that you are calm in any storm and nobody understands why. Quietness means that you are in a position of total control in the middle of a crisis because you know the government of Heaven is above every earthly government. Quietness means you don't start talking loudly when everybody else does. People get all hyper, concerned, and frustrated while you remain calm. Why? You're not under their government. Confidence means you have complete trust in your government. You trust your government to take care of you. Who can say that about any governments on earth?

> *For the kingdom of God is not a matter of eating and drinking, but of righteousness, peace and joy in the Holy Spirit* (Romans 14:17).

Anyone who serves Christ in this way, by obeying the laws and principles of righteousness, will receive the approval of God and man. No one will attack you for doing well. If they do attack you, it is because they do not understand you. In this sick, corrupt, sin-ridden world, righteous living is a mystery to many, even a reason for suspicion. That is why we must always be careful to live upright with honor, honesty, and integrity, so no one will have an excuse to attack us or to defame the name of our King. Live righteously, and joy will fill your days, in spite of what happens around you. The joy of the Lord is not subject to the ways of the world or the whims of circumstance because it originates in another place.

The Kingdom of God operates on righteousness. Righteousness is the scepter of God's throne. It aligns us with the Kingdom government and gives us access to Kingdom benefits. Righteousness guarantees that we will receive all the rights that are ours under Kingdom law. And its results are treasures the world craves: peace, quietness, confidence—and joy unspeakable.

PRINCIPLES

1. Jesus reduced the issues of life to two things: (1) the Kingdom of God and (2) the righteousness of God.

2. Righteousness simply means to be in conformity with the laws of the country.

3. Righteousness means right positioning with the government.

4. Kingdom is the horizontal dimension that deals with *power*: rulership, dominion, and control. It is kingship.

5. Righteousness is the vertical dimension that deals with *position*: relationship, right standing, disposition, and authority. It is priesthood.

6. Righteousness is our relationship with the government. Kingdom is our disposition with the government.

7. Righteousness is the key to abundant Kingdom living.

8. Holiness is a manifestation of righteousness.

9. The pursuit of righteousness is the fundamental operating principle for citizens of the Kingdom of God.

10. Righteousness is its own reward.

11. Righteousness is not only personal but also corporate.

12. Righteousness brings reward and the link between the two is obedience.

13. Righteousness is the solution to poverty.

14. Righteousness guarantees that we will receive all the rights that are ours under Kingdom law.

ENDNOTE

1. W. E. Vine, Merrill F. Unger, and William White, Jr., *Vine's Complete Expository Dictionary of Old and New Testament Words*, (Nashville: Thomas Nelson Publishers, 1984, 1996), Old Testament section, 206.

"Never mistake knowledge for wisdom. One helps you make a living; the other helps you make a life."—Sandra Carey

CHAPTER SIX

RIGHTEOUS POSITIONING: THE KEY TO ABUNDANT KINGDOM LIVING

Most people's lives today are out of alignment with the government of God's Kingdom. Unfortunately, this is also true of many Kingdom citizens. Why? Because instead of pursuing God's priorities of the Kingdom and righteousness, we pursue *things*. No matter how hard we try or how great our desire, the qualities we truly want most in life—peace, quietness, confidence, and joy—always seem to elude our grasp. This is because we have bought into the deception that those qualities can be acquired through the things we possess.

Our lives are out of alignment because we are focused on *possessions* rather than on *position*. For many believers today a great disconnect exists between the promises of the Kingdom and the personal realities of daily experience. Many of us live beyond our means, spending more money than we make. We buy cars too expensive for our budget, houses we can't make the payments on, and designer clothes we can't afford, all in the interests of keeping up with (or showing up) our neighbors. We are neck-deep in debt and always seem to end up with too much month left at the end of the money.

What's the problem? We are obsessed with things. Food is a thing. Water is a thing. A house is a thing. A car is a thing. Money is a thing. All of these are just things, and our pursuit of things is destroying us. Our obsession with things is a hunger we will never satisfy. It will gnaw away at us relentlessly so that the more we get, the hungrier we become. As long as we pursue things, we will never know true peace, contentment, or joy. Somehow we must be delivered from our slavery to things. Deliverance is found in only one place: in pursuit of the Kingdom and righteousness of God.

It is a matter of exchanging one hunger for another. Our hunger for things will never be satisfied. But Jesus said, *"Blessed are those who hunger and thirst for righteousness, for they will be filled"* (Matt. 5:6). How hungry are you? What are you hungry for? Is your hunger for the Kingdom greater than your hunger for things? Do you thirst for righteousness more than you thirst for material prosperity? King David of Israel wrote, *"Delight yourself in the Lord and He will give you the desires of your heart"* (Ps. 37:4). If the Kingdom and righteousness of God are your chief desire and delight, He will take care of everything else.

When Jesus said, *"Blessed are those who hunger and thirst for righteousness,"* He used infinitives, which mean continuing action. If you say, "I'm hungry," or "I'm thirsty," you are referring to a temporary condition that

114

will be satisfied once you have some food or drink. If, however, you say, "I hunger," or "I thirst," you are speaking of continuous desires: you continue to be hungry and you continue to be thirsty.

Imagine being stranded in the desert under the baking sun without food or water. After a couple of days (maybe less), the only thing on your mind is the desire to satisfy your hunger and thirst. Nothing else matters. You are willing to sacrifice anything, give up anything, part with anything, do anything to fill the greatest craving in your heart. Jesus said that this is the kind of all-consuming desire you should have for the Kingdom and righteousness of God. An ancient Hebrew psalmist expressed such desire this way: *"As the deer pants for streams of water, so my soul pants for you, O God. My soul thirsts for God, for the living God. When can I go and meet with God?"* (Ps. 42:1-2).

THE DIVINE DISPOSITION

A continuing hunger and thirst for righteousness positions us to enter into the fullness of Kingdom life. Remember that righteousness is a legal term that means to be in alignment with authority; to be in right standing with the governing power. The key to maintaining that right standing is obedience to the laws of that government. In a kingdom, since the king's word is law, righteousness means fulfilling the king's requirements. Our pursuit of righteousness places us in the right positioning to receive all the rights, resources, blessings, and privileges of the Kingdom that are ours as Kingdom citizens.

In this positioning there is a part we play and a part that God plays. Our part is to obey the laws of the government, thus keeping ourselves in alignment. God's part is to open up to us the resources of Heaven. It is a very simple dynamic. We obey, God opens; we disobey, He closes. As long as we obey the law, we have access. As soon as we disobey—get out of alignment—that access shuts down. This explains why so many believers struggle from day to day, pinching pennies, trying to make ends meet but never seem to have enough, with no peace, joy, or contentment. They are out of alignment with their government and their access to Kingdom resources has been shut off.

Whenever this happens, it is always due to sin, which is breaking the law. The literal meaning of the Greek word for sin in the New Testament is to "miss the mark." It is an archery term that refers to falling short of the target. Sin interrupts our communication with God and shuts down the flow of His resources to us. As the psalmist said, "*If I regard iniquity in my heart, the Lord will not hear*" (Ps. 66:18 NKJV). Iniquity is another word for sin but refers specifically to invisible sin, such as greed, envy, lust, and hatred, and is worse than physical sin. Invisible sin is secret sin, which gives rise to visible sins of action.

Righteous positioning means keeping our hearts pure—clean and uncorrupted by iniquity. If we harbor no secret sins in our heart, there will be nothing to give rise to visible sins. Purity of heart is a critical, indispensable key to abundant Kingdom life. Jesus said, *"Blessed are the pure in heart, for they will see God"* (Matt. 5:8). Literally, this means that the pure in heart will see God in everything. The word heart in this verse means "mind." If our minds are pure, we will see God in everything and in everyone. This is the answer to the problem of greed, or lust, or jealousy, or any kind of impure or improper thought or attitude.

What a challenge to live at such a level in our world today! But that is just the challenge that the King calls His citizens to take up, a challenge that we can meet successfully in His mighty power. But we must choose the path of righteousness and be in the right positioning with regard to our King's requirements. We must be in the position to receive His favor.

THE FRUIT OF RIGHTEOUSNESS

I wrote in the previous chapter that righteousness is its own reward, but that does not mean that it is the only reward. Righteousness bears abundant fruit in our lives. One of these is a spirit of generosity, along with the means and capacity to give generously. Jesus said, *"It is more blessed to give than to receive"* (Acts 20:35b), and Paul reminds us that, *"God loves a cheerful giver"* (2 Cor. 9:7b).

Generosity is a character trait of the righteous, of those who are positioned properly with the government of God. After all, if we own nothing and are merely stewards of God's property, there is no reason why we cannot give freely. And if we are heirs to the Kingdom of God and all its riches, which are infinite, we can give with no fear of running out.

David, in another of his psalms, contrasts the righteous and the wicked: *"The wicked borrow and do not repay, but the righteous give generously; those the Lord blesses will inherit the land, but those he curses will be cut off"* (Ps. 37:21-22). Righteousness is aligning ourselves with God's character and nature. In this way we grow to become like Him, and He is a giver. Because God is a giver, when we get into right positioning with Him, He will give us more than we know what to do with. And because we are becoming like Him, we cannot help but become generous givers also.

The prosperity of the righteous is an ongoing blessing from God that spans generations. A few verses later in the same psalm, David writes, *"I was young and now I am old, yet I have never seen the righteous forsaken or their children begging bread. They are always generous and lend freely; their children will be blessed"* (Ps. 37:25-26). God never forsakes the righteous or their children. He always provides for them. The fruit of the righteous extends even beyond their lifetime to bless their children. Righteous living will bear the fruit in our lives of an inheritance we can leave to our descendents. We should be so blessed that our children, grandchildren, nieces, nephews, and cousins should inherit a multiplied blessing, all because we lived our life rightly positioned with God's government. That is the kind of fruit He wants to give us.

Right positioning places us under the protection of the King, who will preserve us even when the wicked are destroyed: *"For the Lord loves the just and will not forsake his faithful ones. They will be protected forever, but the offspring of the wicked will be cut off; the righteous will inherit the land and dwell in it forever"* (Ps. 37:28-29). Ultimately, the real estate of the Kingdom is reserved for the righteous, for those who are lined up with the Kingdom government. The destiny and prosperity of the ancient Israelites were intimately connected to the land. Even today, the only true material wealth of any lasting value, particularly as an inheritance to pass on, is real estate. A fancy house doesn't matter. A fancy car doesn't matter. The best designer label clothes don't matter. These things rust, rot, and fall apart. If you want to leave your children and grandchildren a valuable legacy, leave them land, not things. Leave them also the legacy of your example of not laying up treasures on earth, which pass away, but treasures in Heaven, which last forever (see Matt. 6:19-20).

Not only will the righteous inherit land to dwell in forever, but that land will be covered by a peace and security that the world knows nothing about: *"The fruit of righteousness will be peace; the effect of righteousness will be quietness and confidence forever. My people will live in peaceful dwelling places, in secure homes, in undisturbed places of rest"* (Isa. 32:17-18). What an incredible threefold promise!

First, if we are righteous, we will enjoy the fruit of peace. Why? Because we are not living for the pursuit of

119

things anymore. Our insatiable hunger for things robs us of peace. Peace in this sense means the absence of frustration and worry. Does that describe your life? Are you at peace?

Second, peace will produce the corollary effect of quietness, or calm disposition, even in trouble. Nothing will disturb us. Do you have a calm, quiet disposition no matter what happens?

Third, peace also produces confidence—total trust and faith in the care, provision, and protection of God's government. This means that we can go to sleep at night free of worry, fear, and uncertainty because we know that our King has us covered. Do you have that kind of confidence on an ongoing basis?

"Peaceful dwelling places." "Secure homes." "Undisturbed places of rest." Who wouldn't give anything they had for that kind of peace and security! Yet this is the guaranteed inheritance of the righteous!

Unlike religion, which focuses on externals, life in the Kingdom of God focuses on inner transformation that manifests in external ways. As Paul reminded the believers in Rome, *"For the kingdom of God is not a matter of eating and drinking, but of righteousness, peace and joy in the Holy Spirit, because anyone who serves Christ in this way is pleasing to God and approved by men"* (Rom. 14:17-18). Here we have another amazing promise. One of the fruits of right positioning is that we please God and receive the approval of other people.

Pleasing God should be our focus rather than pleasing people, because when we are pleasing to God, He causes the approval of people to fall upon us. People approving of us does not necessarily mean they will like us. It may be simply that they see a righteous and honorable quality to our lives that they cannot help but respect, and a calm and joyous demeanor in the way we face everyday life that they cannot help but admire and envy. Our righteousness brings pleasure to God and elicits, however grudgingly, the respect and approval of people.

Righteousness, then, is the primary key to Kingdom living.

KNOW YOUR CONSTITUTION

Knowledge is the key to everything in life, and it is no different with righteousness. The key to righteousness is knowledge of the law. How can we obey the law if we don't know it? That is why it is so important for us to study the laws of the government under whose authority we live. As Kingdom citizens we live under the King's government, and His Word is law. Since the Bible is the written code of law for the Kingdom of God, it is incumbent upon us as citizens to read it, study it, and know it. We need to know the laws of our Kingdom so we can stay in sync with them and in right positioning with the King. Moreover, knowledge of the Bible will also help us come to know the King Himself—His heart and mind and will and ways and thoughts—which is even more important.

Knowledge of the Bible, our Kingdom constitution, is also the key to effective citizenship in the Kingdom. Most people in any given nation do not know most of the laws of their country. Ignorance of one's constitution is dangerous in at least two ways. First, ignorance of the law can lead to inadvertent violation of the law, resulting in legal penalties and loss of alignment with the government (unrighteousness). How can we obey what we don't know to obey? Second, ignorance of the law usually means also ignorance of one's rights under the law. If we don't know what our citizen rights are, how can we claim them? So ignorance of the law means that we lose twice.

The same thing is true in the Kingdom of God. If we don't know our constitution, the Word of God, we will not be able to obey it or claim our constitutional rights as Kingdom citizens. In fact, the Bible itself states that it exists for the specific purpose of training us for Kingdom living: *"All scripture is God-breathed and is useful for teaching, rebuking, correcting and training in righteousness,"* (2 Tim. 3:16). God gave us His Word so we can learn how to live in His Kingdom. Righteous living does not come naturally, even for Kingdom citizens. We must train our minds so we can walk in the things of God and discipline our bodies to do the right thing. If we know what to do every day, we will know also how to do it right. The Bible is the constitution of the Kingdom of God and the source of righteousness for its citizens.

Let's take this one step further. Knowledge of the constitution and principles of the Kingdom is vital for us as Kingdom citizens, but just as vital is our need to stand boldly and firmly for them before the world. The people of the world are looking for the Kingdom, but how will they learn of it if we keep silent? King David understood this, which is why he wrote:

> *I desire to do your will, O my God; your law is within my heart. I proclaim righteousness in the great assembly; I do not seal my lips, as You know, O Lord. I do not hide Your righteousness in my heart; I speak of Your faithfulness and salvation. I do not conceal Your love and Your truth from the great assembly* (Psalm 40:8-10).

Remember, now, David was not a priest; he was the king. His was the world of politics, warfare, government and administration. David undoubtedly met regularly with the ministers, administrators, and other lower-level officials of his kingdom to conduct the regular affairs of kingdom life and operation. In addition, as king he no doubt received from time to time official delegations from other kingdoms in the region. Yet, according to these verses, David never hesitated, even on these official occasions, to speak of righteousness and the faithfulness and salvation of God. They were as much a part of his life and his rule as breathing.

Many people insist that we should never mix faith and politics. Such a concept would have been completely foreign to David. He was a man after God's own heart and he never shrank back from telling anyone within earshot of the glories, mercy, love, power, and majesty of the Lord. There were also certain things he simply would not do out of love and obedience to his God. He would make his position plain to everyone and then say, "Here is where I stand."

How we need today believing politicians and CEOs and managers and supervisors and employees who will stand up for righteousness and say, "Here is where I stand!" We need people who will say, "I will not cheat, I will not lie, I will not cut corners, I will not accept bribes, I will not take kickbacks, I will not pad invoices, I will not steal time from my employer, because all of these things violate my higher law, the law of Heaven."

We need people who will say, "I will pursue honor, honesty, integrity, and excellence in everything I do because these keep me in right positioning with my King." If you get fired for your stand, so what? God has you covered. He honors, protects, and rewards the righteous. Jesus said, *"Blessed are those who are persecuted because of righteousness, for theirs is the kingdom of Heaven"* (Matt. 5:10). Stand up for righteousness and God will bless you with the whole Kingdom.

POSITIONING IS ESSENTIAL FOR KINGDOM LIFE

Positioning places us under proper authority in the Kingdom. This concept is so important that even Jesus had to get into position before He began His public ministry. One day Jesus came to the Jordan River, where the prophet John the Baptist was baptizing people for repentance (renouncing and turning away) of sin. Jesus stepped into the water to be baptized.

> But John tried to deter Him, saying, "I need to be baptized by You, and do You come to me?" Jesus replied, "Let it be so now; it is proper for us to do this to fulfill all righteousness." Then John consented (Matthew 3:14-15).

As the Son of God, Jesus was without sin and did not need to be baptized for repentance of sin. And John clearly recognized Jesus as being greater than he. Why then did Jesus say, "Let it be so now" in order "to fulfill all righteousness"? In essence, He was saying to John, "This is not a matter of greatness, but a matter of positioning. According to the law of the Lord, you are the one with authority on earth right now. I have to get under you. It's not a matter of what you think or who I am, but a matter of my positioning. I have to be in alignment with My Father, and you, John, are the alignment. I have to get under you in order for Me to be under Myself."

If Jesus Christ, who was God in the flesh, had to submit to the authority He established, who are we to think that we don't? Our protection is submission to Kingdom authority, positioning ourselves in alignment to the Word and will of the King.

Jesus' decision to position Himself by being baptized by John was obviously the right decision, as is borne out by what happened next:

As soon as Jesus was baptized, He went up out of the water. At that moment Heaven was opened, and He saw the Spirit of God descending like a dove and lighting on Him. And a voice from Heaven said, "This is My Son, whom, I love; with Him I am well pleased" (Matthew 3:16-17).

Remember, righteousness is pleasing to God, and righteousness means positioning ourselves under His authority.

Righteous positioning, which is based on obedience, is so important that it is the standard of measure in the Kingdom of God. So important, in fact, as to prompt Jesus to issue this warning:

Anyone who breaks one of the least of these commandments and teaches others to do the same will be called least in the kingdom of Heaven, but whoever practices and teaches these commands will be called great in the kingdom of Heaven. For I tell you that unless your righteousness surpasses that of the Pharisees and the teachers of the law, you will certainly not enter the kingdom of Heaven (Matthew 5:19-20).

Greatness in the Kingdom of Heaven is measured by the standard of obedience to the King's commands, which are the law. Those who obey are called great while those who disobey are called least. In the eyes of the people of Jesus' day (as well as in their own eyes), the Pharisees and teachers of the law were "great" because they were committed to exact observance of the Jewish law.

Strictly speaking, no one was more obedient to the letter of the law than the Pharisees and teachers of the law.

The problem, however, was that these leaders approached the law and righteousness from a religious mind-set. They were seeking righteousness according to their own merit. They thought that strict obedience to the law in every minute detail would earn them favor with God. In truth, however, they were never aligned with God's law. They were never in tune with His heart and mind. They were out of position because they sought righteousness through religion.

Religion will never line us up with God. Jesus did not bring a religion when He came. He brought the good news that the Kingdom of Heaven had come to earth. We don't become righteous by lining up with religion. We become righteous by positioning ourselves according to the laws and principles of the Kingdom of Heaven. It doesn't matter how many rituals we perform, how many worship services we attend or how often we go to prayer meeting; without deliberate and conscious aligning of ourselves with Kingdom authority, all the rest means nothing. Except our righteousness exceeds that of religion and man-made tradition, we will never enter the Kingdom of Heaven.

Religion doesn't work. We see it in the lives of believers all the time. Believers who are trapped in the "religion" of institutionalized Christianity, with all of its man-made trappings and having "*a form of godliness but denying its power*" (2 Tim. 3:5), do not position themselves according to the principles of the Kingdom. Consequently, they do not enjoy the fruits and benefits of Kingdom life. This is why so many believers are broke, destitute, and struggling, and living with the same fears, worries, and sicknesses as the rest of the world.

It is time for all of us who are believers to get real with God and do what He says. He has promised that if we will obey His laws and pursue righteous positioning with Him, He will add everything else to us.

Righteousness for Reconciliation

The fundamental and universal need of every human being on earth is righteousness. God's Word makes it clear that none of us are righteous in and of ourselves:

> The fool says in his heart, "There is no God." They are corrupt, their deeds are vile; there is no one who does good. The Lord looks down from Heaven on the sons of men to see if there are any who understand, any who seek God. All have turned aside, they have together become corrupt; there is no one who does good, not even one (Psalm 14:1-3).

Sin and moral corruption are universal, a legacy of Adam and Eve's disobedience in the Garden of Eden. Furthermore, there is nothing any of us can do to make ourselves righteous: "*All of us have become like one who is unclean, and all our righteous acts are like filthy rags; we all shrivel up like a leaf, and like the wind our sins sweep us away*" (Isa. 64:6). Unless righteousness comes to us from an outside source, we have no hope of entering the Kingdom of God.

Fortunately for our sake, God Himself has provided the righteousness we all so desperately need: "*For in the gospel a righteousness from God is revealed, a righteousness that is by faith from first to last, just as it is written: 'The righteous will live by faith'*" (Rom. 1:17). The word gospel means "good news." Jesus came preaching the gospel of the Kingdom of Heaven. As this verse from Paul's letter to the Romans indicates, the gospel of the Kingdom had within it a "righteousness from God" that is appropriated by faith. Faith in Christ and in His death on the Cross to remove our sin and moral corruption activates the righteousness of God and applies it to our lives. So when we come into right positioning with God's government in the Kingdom, it is not our righteousness but His in which we stand.

"The righteous will live by faith." This means that they believe the Word of the Kingdom government. Our righteousness comes from God. He is saying to us, "Look, either you can position yourself (which is what religion tries to do) or you can allow Me to position you. Religion is weak and useless; it avails nothing. Only in My Kingdom can you find righteousness. You could not save yourself so I saved you. You could not clean up your own mess so I cleaned it up for you. Through the blood of My Son I washed away your sin and moral defilement. It is I who put you back into right alignment with My government.

I am the one who restored your right standing. You are in the right position because I put you there."

To put an even finer point on it, Jesus Christ Himself is our righteousness. It is through Him that the righteousness of God becomes our own:

> *It is because of Him* [God] *that you are in Christ Jesus, who has become for us wisdom from God— that is, our righteousness, holiness and redemption. Therefore, as it is written: "Let him who boasts boast in the Lord"* (1 Corinthians 1:30-31).

Jesus became for us our righteousness, holiness, and redemption. We owe everything to Him. That is why we have no right or reason to boast in ourselves or in our own goodness. We should boast in the Lord alone, who has brought us back into right positioning with Himself and given us access to the Kingdom of God and all its riches, resources, and privileges. From our position of righteousness, which we have from Him, we can confidently anticipate that He will meet and supply all our needs. Religion will never do this.

People outside the Kingdom use religion to try to establish a righteousness of their own making because they are ignorant of the righteousness that is available from God. Paul expressed it this way:

> *Since they did not know the righteousness that comes from God and sought to establish their own, they did not submit to God's righteousness. Christ is the end*

of the law so that there may be righteousness for everyone who believes (Romans 10:3-4).

Christ is the end of the law. He is the end of all of the rituals and laws people try to keep. He is the end of all of our self-effort to become righteous. He is the end of all our attempts to relate to God on our own terms. For everyone who believes—everyone who trusts and submits their lives to Him—Jesus becomes their righteousness. This is why we all need Jesus in our lives. Only through Him can we become rightly positioned with God.

The righteousness we receive in Christ is not for ourselves alone. When we become rightly positioned with the government of God, He commissions us to spread the word of His righteousness to others so they too may become rightly positioned with Him. This commission is called the ministry of reconciliation:

Therefore, if anyone is in Christ, he is a new creation; the old has gone, the new has come! All this is from God, who reconciled us to Himself through Christ and gave us the ministry of reconciliation: that God was in Christ reconciling the world to Himself in Christ, not counting men's sins against them. And He has committed to us the message of reconciliation. We are therefore Christ's ambassadors, as though God were making His appeal through us. We implore you on Christ's behalf: Be reconciled to God. God made Him who had no sin to be sin for us, so that in Him we might become the righteousness of God (2 Corinthians 5:17-21).

To *reconcile* means "to restore a broken relationship, remove an estrangement, or bring back into balance." All of these describe what happens when we become the righteousness of God in Christ: our broken relationship with God is restored, the wall of separation between us is removed, and our lives are brought back into the balance God originally intended. We are placed in right positioning. And from that right and secure place we are prepared and equipped to carry the message of the Kingdom to others so they too can be reconciled to God. This is the good news of the Kingdom!

PRINCIPLES

1. Our pursuit of righteousness places us in the right positioning to receive all the rights, resources, blessings, and privileges of the Kingdom that are ours as Kingdom citizens.

2. Purity of heart is a critical, indispensable key to abundant Kingdom life.

3. The prosperity of the righteous is an ongoing blessing from God that spans generations.

4. Right positioning places us under the protection of the King.

5. The key to righteousness is knowledge of the law.

6. Knowledge of the Bible, our Kingdom constitution, is also the key to effective citizenship in the Kingdom.

7. The Bible is the constitution of the Kingdom of God and the source of righteousness for its citizens.

8. Positioning places us under proper authority in the Kingdom.

9. Righteous positioning, which is based on obedience, is so important that it is the standard of measure in the Kingdom of God.

10. Our righteousness comes from God.

11. Jesus Christ Himself is our righteousness.

12. When we become rightly positioned with the government of God, He commissions us to spread the word of His righteousness to others so they too may become rightly positioned with Him.

"Life contains but two tragedies. One is not to get your hearts desire; the other is to get it."—George Bernard Shaw

CHAPTER SEVEN

THE BENEFITS
OF RIGHTEOUSNESS

Have you ever wondered, "What's the use of being righteous?" What good does it do to try to live right and do the right thing? After all, it often seems as though the people who live only for themselves get along better than anybody else. They lie and cheat, they follow dishonest and unscrupulous business practices, yet they always seem to prosper. In the meantime, honest, hard-working people labor day after day just for the daily food on their table. If righteousness is so important, why do the wicked prosper?

This is an age-old question. An ancient Hebrew psalmist named Asaph asked the same thing. When he saw evil men do well, it made him question why he tried so hard to live right:

> *But as for me, my feet had almost slipped; I had nearly lost my foothold. For I envied the arrogant when I saw the prosperity of the wicked. They have no struggles; their bodies are healthy and strong. They are free from the burdens common to man; they are not plagued by human ills...This is what the*

wicked are like—always carefree, they increase in wealth. Surely in vain have I kept my heart pure; in vain have I washed my hands in innocence. All day long I have been plagued; I have been punished every morning (Psalm 73:2-5, 12-14).

Asaph was so troubled over this that he almost gave up. He almost abandoned his attempt to live righteously, until the day he received a revelation from God. When he began to see things from the vantage point of the Kingdom of Heaven, his entire perspective changed:

When I tried to understand all this, it was oppressive to me till I entered the sanctuary of God; then I understood their final destiny. Surely you place them on slippery ground; you cast them down to ruin. How suddenly they are destroyed, completely swept away by terrors! As a dream when one awakes, so when you arise, O Lord, you will despise them as fantasies (Psalm 73:16-20).

Things look different when viewed from a Kingdom perspective. Unrighteous people who so often appear to us to be stable, successful, healthy, wealthy, and trouble-free are actually on a slippery slope toward destruction. Their stability is only apparent, not real. As it says in another psalm, the wicked *"are like chaff that the wind blows away"* (Ps. 1:4b). They are here one day and gone the next.

It is a different story with the righteous. The same psalm says of the righteous person, *"But his delight is in the law of the Lord, and on His law he meditates day and night. He is like a tree planted by streams of water, which yields its fruit in season and whose leaf does not wither. Whatever he does prospers"* (Ps. 1:2-3). The psalm concludes with a powerful contrast: *"For the Lord watches over the way of the righteous, but the way of the wicked will perish"* (Ps. 1:6). Which would you rather be, chaff blown away by the wind or a tree firmly planted, well nourished, and prosperous?

So what good is righteousness? It gives us true stability, success, health, wealth that lasts, and positions us to overcome all the troubles that life throws our way.

Even though the righteousness we receive in Christ is not given for us alone but also for the purpose of the ministry of reconciliation, righteousness does bring with it significant personal benefits.

SEED FOR THE SOWER

You read in Chapter Six that one of the fruits of righteousness—one of its by-products in our lives—is a spirit of generosity. A giving spirit is second nature to the righteous because righteousness molds us into the likeness of God, who is a generous giver. Giving is also a fundamental principle with regard to the benefits of righteousness because what we receive is proportional to what we give. The more we give, and the greater the generosity with which we give, the more we will receive in return. Jesus said, *"Give, and it will be given to you. A good measure, pressed down, shaken together and running over, will be poured into your lap. For with the measure you use, it will be measured to you"* (Luke 6:38).

When we start to give as God gives, He gives us even more in return. That is what Jesus meant when He said, *"a good measure, pressed down, shaken together and running over."* The King of Heaven is not stingy with His treasures. No one can outgive God.

Every time we give generously in the Spirit of Christ as Kingdom citizens, we lay up for ourselves treasures in Heaven, as Jesus said, *"where moth and rust do not destroy, and where thieves do not break in and steal"* (Matt. 6:20b). One common biblical metaphor for giving is the image of sowing seed. Whenever we sow seeds of generosity we are setting ourselves up for a harvest of greater righteousness and prosperity:

> *Whoever sows sparingly will also reap sparingly, and whoever sows generously will also reap generously. Each man should give what he has decided in his heart to give, not reluctantly or under compulsion, for God loves a cheerful giver. And God is able to make all grace abound to you, so that in all things at all times, having all that you need, you will abound in every good work…Now he who supplies seed to the sower and bread for food will also supply and increase your store of seed and will enlarge the harvest of your righteousness. You will be made rich in every way so that you can be generous on every occasion…*(2 Corinthians 9:6-8, 10-11a).

Generous sowing will reap a bountiful harvest. A farmer who is stingy with his seed will realize only a tiny return. God gives seed to the sower. This is an important principle. You must be a sower if you want to attract seed. It is no good trying to wait, saying, "I'll sow once I have plenty of seed." No! Sow now with whatever seed you have and the Seed Supplier will give you more. The seed you receive and the increase you experience are linked to your generosity. Increase and prosperity are not given for us to consume ourselves but that we might be generous toward others. Once again it is the issue of stewardship versus ownership.

As you give generously, God will also increase the harvest of your righteousness because giving brings you into alignment with Him. He will strengthen your right standing and firmly anchor your positioning. Every time you sow you line yourself up with God, who then gives you more seed to sow, enabling you to stay lined up even as you continue to sow generously toward others. According to these Scriptures, God's desire and intention is to make you *"rich in every way so that you can be generous on every occasion."* Have you ever wished you could contribute to a worthy cause or project but could not because you lacked the means? God wants to bring you to the place where you *can* give on *every* occasion.

As far as God is concerned, everything He gives you is a seed. In fact, seeds are all He gives. Seeds have virtually unlimited potential but they must be sown in order for their potential to be released. God gives you seed to see what you will do with it. If you hoard it and keep it for yourself, it will never sprout, you will never grow and you will miss out on the joys and benefits that come from greater righteousness and a generous spirit. Sow your seed faithfully, however, and God will replace it with even more seed so you can increase your generosity. Be faithful with a little and He will give you much. And He will continue to do so as long as you use what He gives for His sake and for the sake of others rather than for your own sake.

THE BENEFIT OF THE KING'S FAVOR

Righteousness attracts God because He is righteous. He looks favorably on all who seek to live righteously in faith. Just as people in earthly kingdoms long for the favor of their king, so we too should seek the favor of the King of Heaven. We should look for Him to extend His scepter over us:

> … Your throne, O God, will last forever and ever, and righteousness will be the scepter of your kingdom (Hebrews 1:8).

As you read in Chapter Five, the scepter is a king's symbol of authority. Anyone under the scepter of the king was under his protection and care. None could enter the king's presence unless he first extended his scepter to them. If a king wants to show you favor, he will extend his scepter over you, and the next thing he says becomes law over you. What you were or what you are now do not matter. What happened yesterday is of no account. All that matters is what the king says right now. You could walk into his presence penniless and homeless, hear the king say with extended scepter, "I grant you 10,000 acres of prime woodland and a manor house," and walk out a rich man with a fine home. When you enjoy the favor of the king you don't have to work for what he gives you. He gives because he wants to; that's why it is called *favor*.

Traditionally, a king would hold his scepter in his right hand. The Bible uses similar imagery to refer to God as King. Those under God's favor are said to be at His right hand, while those under His judgment are at his left. If the right hand of the Lord is upon you, it means that He has appointed His authority toward you; He has given you access.

What does this mean in practical terms? Simply this: if you line yourself up with God in righteousness, He will extend His scepter, He will direct His favor toward you and things that you've worked all your life for He will give you in two minutes. That's the power of kingly authority. Authority is better than work. In fact, authority can cancel or override a lifetime of work. A king has authority over his entire kingdom.

The Bible says that the way to get God's authority to work for us is by maintaining righteousness in our lives. That is why Jesus told us to seek first God's Kingdom and His righteousness and *then* everything would be added to us. The righteousness must come before the addition. But when God has decided to add the addition to you, nothing in Heaven or on earth will keep Him from giving it to you.

THE BENEFITS OF UNDERSTANDING AND DISCERNMENT

The pursuit of righteousness is the secret to maturity, understanding, and discernment in Kingdom living. Lack of righteousness in our lives leads to misalignment with God and stunts our growth so that we never progress beyond the stage of spiritual toddlers. It is the spiritual equivalent of moving from a milk diet to a solid food diet, as the writer of the Book of Hebrews explains:

> *Anyone who lives on milk, being still an infant, is not acquainted with the teaching about righteousness. But solid food is for the mature, who by constant use have trained themselves to distinguish good from evil* (Hebrews 5:13-14).

People who are not experiencing the benefits of Kingdom life are like little children who are still living on milk, not having yet progressed to solid food. And, in fact, they cannot progress. Just as the digestive system of an infant cannot handle solid food, the mind of an immature believer cannot handle the "solid" demands of righteousness.

If we never seriously commit ourselves to pursue a life of righteousness, we will never mature; we will remain spiritual babies all our lives. Only those committed to righteousness will reach maturity. They alone will know the riches and joy of Kingdom life lived to the full. A life of mature righteousness also carries a strong protective element because it brings discernment of right and wrong, helping us to embrace the first and reject the second.

One of the biggest problems plaguing much of the Western Church today is that believers are not being taught the importance of personal righteousness in daily life. Consequently, many of them do not know how to align their lives with God or how to tell when they are out of alignment. As a result, they do not experience the blessings, benefits, provision, or prosperity of the Kingdom because their unrighteous lifestyle has shut down their access to these things.

Among other things, God desires every citizen of His Kingdom to be financially free. This does not mean never having any bills, but rather always having the means to pay them on time. Wealth in the Kingdom of God is not storing things up, but always having access to everything. Whenever we need something, it's there. There is no need we have that is too big for God to meet.

As believers and Kingdom citizens, we have a "pipeline" to the supply chain of Heaven. God uses this pipeline to meet our every need, physical or spiritual. But our pipeline must be clean, clear, and open, and righteousness is what keeps it that way. The pipeline is always open from God's end. Our lifestyle determines whether or not it remains open at our end. Living righteously keeps our end clear.

THE BENEFITS OF GOD'S PROTECTION AND PROMOTION

When we actively pursue righteousness in our daily living in obedience to Christ's command, we enjoy a level of security and protection that those outside the Kingdom of God do not have. This does not mean we never face trouble or difficulty or negative circumstances—these are an inescapable part of living in a sin-corrupted world. It does mean, however, that even during such times—and especially during such times—the favor of our King rests upon us and He delivers us safely and triumphantly through. And the watching world will be amazed, wondering not only how we survived but also how we came out on top.

Why are we so secure? Because the Lord never takes His eyes off of us: *"He does not take his eyes off the righteous; He enthrones them with kings and exalts them forever"* (Job 36:7). Not only does God protect us; He also lifts us up. Under God's protection and favor we do more than cope with life. He enables us to overcome every obstacle and meet every challenge so that we live life to the fullest. This verse says that God exalts the righteous. That means if we stay right with God, He will promote us in every situation we go into. We will rise to the top and no one will understand why.

In the world, promotion often depends on whose back you scratch, whose palm you grease, whose ego you stroke, or whose bed you sleep in. Getting ahead is dog-eat-dog, cutthroat competition where anything goes as long as it works. Promotion in the Kingdom comes from above—from the King Himself—and rests on His favor as well as correct alignment through the pursuit of righteousness.

The key to promotion by the King is to keep our pipeline clear of any obstructions. This means working hard to keep ourselves in line with God and avoiding anything that will move us out of position. Don't lie, don't cheat, don't curse and don't covet. Let go of anger, envy, and jealousy. Be quick to forgive and always ready to extend mercy. Treat everyone with kindness, dignity, and respect. Love everyone, even enemies. Always return good, even to those who are hostile or hateful.

We often have little or no control over what comes into our lives or how people act toward us but we always have control over how we respond. Keeping our pipeline clear is up to us; God will not do it for us. He will not force us to live righteously. But unless we do, we will never experience the benefits and blessings that righteousness brings.

God's protection is linked closely with His favor, like two sides of the same coin. King David of Israel was familiar with this connection:

> *Let all who take refuge in you be glad; let them ever sing for joy. Spread your protection over them, that those who love your name may rejoice in you. For surely, O Lord, you bless the righteous; you surround them with your favor as with a shield* (Psalm 5:11-12).

God's favor surrounds the righteous like a shield. A shield, of course, is a defensive weapon that protects the user by deflecting and turning aside the attack of an enemy. When God's favor surrounds us, nothing harmful can get through to us; we are perfectly safe in His presence. When God's favor surrounds us, everything that He desires for us will come to pass.

Do you want to live under God's protection and favor? Then commit yourself consciously and deliberately to think and live righteously according to the laws of God's Kingdom. If you do, then no evil planned against you will succeed. Nothing will be able to touch you except what the Lord allows. Your business will flourish while others' are struggling. A way will be made for you where no way seemed possible. You will experience abundant provision when others around you are suffering shortages. At the right moment in God's timing He will exalt you, seemingly overnight in the eyes of many watching.

The best biblical illustration of this is found in the story of Joseph from the Book of Genesis. Sold into slavery by his jealous brothers, Joseph spent many years as the slave of the captain of the guard to Pharaoh, where he distinguished himself by his ability and incorruptible integrity. God prospered Joseph so that he was placed in charge of his master's entire household. Joseph's integrity cost him a heavy price. When he refused to sleep with his master's wife at her invitation, she retaliated by accusing him of attempted rape, which landed him in prison. Even there, however, God blessed him and he once again rose to leadership even among the other prisoners.

Finally, the day came when Joseph had the chance to interpret a dream that Pharaoh had, a dream that prophesied seven years of plenty followed by seven years of famine. The pharaoh, recognizing Joseph's peerless integrity and character, promoted him on the spot from slave to prime minister. In a moment, Joseph was elevated from prisoner in the dungeon to second-in-command in all of Egypt. And from his new position, Joseph was directly responsible for preserving the lives of countless thousands of people, including his own father and brothers, during the severe years of famine that followed. Joseph's time had arrived and God exalted him. But if Joseph had not been faithful in pursuing and living in righteousness all those years, his elevation probably would never have happened.

Many people today, including many believers, blame "the system" for their troubles. It is time for believers everywhere to get out from under "the system" in their thinking and behavior and get under the Kingdom of God and its laws. All the Lord asks us to do is seek first His Kingdom and His righteousness and, system or no system, He will add everything else to us. If you are a believer and a follower of Christ, you are not a victim of your job or of the system. On the contrary, if you will diligently pursue righteousness in your daily life, He will bless you in spite of your job and in spite of the system and, because of your presence there, even bless the company you work for.

Righteousness is such a strong shield that it protects even in the face of disaster. The Bible says that God will not destroy the righteous along with the wicked. So the presence of even one righteous person is enough to protect all the unrighteous people around him or her. Once again, Joseph's experience is a good example. Joseph may have been the only righteous person in Egypt, yet God preserved the entire nation through Joseph and because of Joseph.

Being under the protection and favor of God means not only that He watches over us but also that He listens to what we say. When we pursue and walk in righteousness, God focuses His eyes and ears on us: *"The eyes of the Lord are on the righteous and His ears are attentive to their cry"* (Ps. 34:15). The Bible assures us that we can be completely confident that when God hears us, He will answer us:

> *This is the confidence we have in approaching God: that if we ask anything according to His will, He hears us. And if we know that He hears us—whatever we ask—we know that we have what we have asked of Him* (1 John 5:14-15).

Asking "according to His will" means not only asking in agreement with God's will but also asking from the place of righteous positioning, because righteousness is always God's will. We have the clear promise that whenever we pray from the position of righteousness, God will answer and give us what we have asked of Him. This is perhaps one of the most important reasons of all for us to be careful to do nothing that will bring us out of alignment with God and interfere with our relationship with Him.

THE BENEFIT OF DELIVERANCE

God not only hears and answers the righteous when they call, but He also delivers them from and through the difficulties of life:

> *The righteous cry out, and the Lord hears them; He delivers them from all their troubles. The Lord is close to the brokenhearted and saves those who are crushed in spirit. A righteous man may have many troubles, but the Lord delivers him from them all; He protects all his bones, not one of them will be broken. Evil will slay the wicked; the foes of the righteous will be condemned. The Lord redeems His servants; no one will be condemned who takes refuge in Him* (Psalm 34:17-22).

As long as we are aligned with God, He will deliver us from *all* our troubles. This does not mean that we will never experience trouble in life, but it does mean that we can trust God to carry us through and give us the strength and the grace to prevail. He won't leave us to fend for ourselves.

Notice that verse 20 promises that God will protect the "bones" of the righteous so that none of them will be broken. David, the psalmist, is speaking metaphorically here. This is not a promise for protection against literal broken bones. The word *bones* here refers to the framework that holds everything together, like the human skeleton forms the framework that holds the body together. The promise of this verse, then, is that God will bless and deliver the righteous by making sure that the framework of their lives never falls apart. God's promise to the righteous is, "I will keep your frame intact!" Even when the lives of others around us are falling apart, God will preserve our frame and that of our family.

Jesus promised that the house built on a solid foundation would stand through all the storms (Matt. 7:24-25). Righteousness is a fundamental part of the solid foundation on which we must build our lives if we are to withstand the storm. God's promise to protect our bones is a promise to protect us from being blown away by the forces of life that may destroy others. As long as we pursue righteousness and seek to stay in alignment with Him, God will hold us up.

THE BENEFIT OF PROSPERITY

Righteousness is also the key to prosperity. Although the Bible does not teach a "prosperity gospel" or a "name-it-and-claim-it" theology, as some teach, it does promise prosperity as a reward for the righteous:

Misfortune pursues the sinner, but prosperity is the reward of the righteous. A good man leaves an inheritance for his children's children, but a sinner's wealth is stored up for the righteous (Proverbs 13:21-22).

Prosperity, as the word is used here, includes but is not limited to material wealth. In fact, the meaning of the word goes much deeper to cover overall quality and fruitfulness of life. The life of the righteous will be full, abundant, and fruitful in every sense and in every dimension. In contrast, sinners (the unrighteous) will face misfortune after misfortune.

As I said before, the health, wealth, and stability of the wicked are only apparent, not real. As quickly as a heartbeat they can all be stripped away. Righteousness, however, brings rewards that will not tarnish or rust away but instead will endure forever.

The wealth of sinners is being stored up for the righteous. Many people have claimed this verse but have not seen it fulfilled for them. Why? Because they claimed it while ignoring the precondition of righteousness. Only those who actively pursue righteousness and seek to live according to God's will have the right to claim this verse. Righteousness is the requirement; the wealth of the wicked is the reward. As Lord of the universe and owner of all that is, God will see to it in the end that the wealth and treasure of His Kingdom end up in the hands of righteous people who can be trusted to exercise mature, faithful stewardship.

Rewarding the righteous is the just thing to do in a just Kingdom ruled by a just God: *"Surely the righteous still are rewarded; surely there is a God who judges the earth"* (Ps. 58:11b). This verse says, in other words, that as long as there is a living God who judges the earth, the righteous will be rewarded. It is a principle as certain as God's Word and as permanent as eternity. There really is a reward for clean living.

Unlike the unrighteous, who will wither and be blown away like chaff in the wind, the righteous will flourish and remain fruitful for a lifetime:

The righteous will flourish like a palm tree, they will grow like a cedar of Lebanon; planted in the house of the Lord, they will flourish in the courts of our God. They will still bear fruit in old age, they will stay fresh and green, proclaiming, *"The Lord is upright; He is my Rock, and there is no wickedness in Him"* (Psalm 92:12-15).

Judging from these verses, the righteous are not supposed to die old and crippled! They are supposed to remain of sound mind and body, bearing fruit well into old age. The phrase, *"they will stay fresh and green,"* refers to the idea that righteousness should keep us young in heart and mind no matter our physical age. Righteousness will help us maintain our zest for life right up to the end. And our witness to the greatness and righteousness of God should be just as strong, and even stronger, at the end of our days as at any other time in life.

God's Plumb Line

Finally, righteousness benefits us by protecting us from the judgment of God. Righteousness is the essential standard by which God will judge the world. If we are already living and walking there, we are safe.

> *This is what the Sovereign Lord says: "See, I lay a stone in Zion, a tested stone, a precious cornerstone for a sure foundation; the one who trusts will never be dismayed. I will make justice the measuring line and righteousness the plumb line* (Isaiah 28:16-17a).

A plumb line is a weighted string that is used in construction work to make sure that walls are straight when they are erected. If the wall line from top to bottom is parallel to the plumb line, the wall is said to be "true to plumb." That means that it is in line with the standard of measure.

In the Kingdom of God, righteousness is the plumb line God uses to measure whether or not our lives are "true to plumb" or whether we are out of alignment. The standard of measure cannot be adjusted; it reveals what has to be. Pursuing righteousness means that we adjust our lives, attitudes, and behavior until we fall within God's standard of measure. Once we do, we are properly aligned with Him, properly positioned for full abundance and fruitfulness and to enjoy fully all the benefits and rewards that come with Kingdom life.

The Kingdom of God has everything we could ever possibly need or want. And the Lord wants us to have and enjoy them all; but our lives must be true to plumb. Being born again is not enough by itself. It is the necessary first step because it gets us into the Kingdom, but our access to Kingdom wealth and resources grows as we grow in practical righteousness.

How do you measure up? If God dropped His plumb line alongside your life today, where would you fall? Would your life be out of alignment or would you be true to plumb?

PRINCIPLES

1. What we receive is proportional to what we give.

2. When you enjoy the favor of the King you don't have to work for what He gives you.

3. The pursuit of righteousness is the secret to maturity, understanding, and discernment in Kingdom living.

4. Only those committed to righteousness will reach maturity.

5. When we actively pursue righteousness in our daily living in obedience to Christ's command, we enjoy a level of security and protection that those outside the Kingdom of God do not have.

6. If we stay right with God, He will promote us in every situation we go into.

7. When God's favor surrounds us, everything that He desires for us will come to pass.

8. Righteousness is such a strong shield that it protects even in the face of disaster.

9. Being under the protection and favor of God means not only that He watches over us but also that He listens to what we say.

10. As long as we are aligned with God, He will deliver us from *all* our troubles.

11. Righteousness is the key to prosperity.

12. Righteousness benefits us by protecting us from the judgment of God.

13. Pursuing righteousness means that we adjust our lives, attitudes, and behavior until we fall within God's standard of measure.

*"He who gets his personal worth
from the things he possesses must be
sure to never lose his possessions."*

CHAPTER EIGHT

THE KINGDOM KEY TO ACCESSING THE THINGS OF THE KINGDOM

One reason the concept of the Kingdom of Heaven is so hard for many people to grasp at first is because understanding it calls for a complete change of thinking. Moving from a worldly view to a Kingdom view requires a total paradigm shift. Priorities in the Kingdom are different from those in the world. Worth and value are assigned differently. Many of the things the world values most are regarded as worthless in the Kingdom of Heaven. Standards for evaluating greatness are very different between the world and the Kingdom. The world judges greatness in terms of money, power, and influence, while the Kingdom sees it in humility and self-giving service. And finally, the Kingdom and the world take entirely different views from each other with regard to *things*.

From the worldly point of view, things are an end in themselves. People seek the acquisition of things to satisfy their own selfish desires, to fill the emptiness in their hearts, to impress other people, and to advance their status and standing in the eyes of society. For Kingdom citizens, on the other hand, things are a means to an end, by-products of righteous living to be used not for selfish gratification but to bring blessings to others.

THE SEDUCTIVE POWER OF THINGS

Humankind is motivated, driven, and preoccupied with the pursuit of things. Few things in this world are more seductive to the heart of people than the lure of materialism. People's greed for things is one of the strongest of all motivators of human behavior, often outstripping even the motivators of love and family loyalty. Outside the Kingdom of God virtually every human action can be traced back to a material motivation. The quest for things drives human culture.

Everything we do in life we do in order to get more things. Think about it. Why do people go to work? To maintain their ability to buy things. Why do many of them try to "marry up"? To have access to more things. Why do many people compromise their principles and sleep with the boss? It's not out of love. They are simply trying to gain an advantage and position themselves for more power and more influence, which translate into more money for acquiring more things.

Religion is no help at all because it has been corrupted by the same seduction. "Religious" prayers, which include most of the prayers of many believers, are focused on things. Far too many people regard prayer as little more than a shopping list for God: "God, I want this, Lord, I need that, God, will you please give me this...."

As if materialistic prayers were not bad enough, most people also have a materialistic faith, a faith that is focused on things. Even within the church there are those whose main reason for following Christ is for what they think they can get from Him. Believing in God's provision of our needs is both biblical and admirable, but many within the church have taken that sound concept too far by effectively making things, not Christ, the object of faith. They "believe" for a new car or a new job or a new house. Rather than pursuing the Kingdom and righteousness of God, they have fallen into the trap of pursuing things, even if they are the things of the Kingdom. But as we have already seen, pursuit of things is always the wrong focus.

All human religions are built on the promise of things: a good harvest, the favor of the gods, victory over one's enemies, good health, great wealth, enlightenment, control or manipulation of the environment, etc. "Religious" Christians are the same way except that they rely on Jesus to provide what they want. Instead of looking on Christ and His Kingdom as the desired *end* or goal of their faith, they use Him as merely a *means* to their real end—things.

Humankind as a whole persists in a collective madness by continually pursuing that which will only bring pain, disappointment, dissatisfaction, and destruction. Things are the source of the world's problems. Crime, sickness, depression, jealousy, covetousness, malice, envy, strife, stress—you name it—at the root of all these problems and more lies the lust for things.

Why do thieves steal? They are after things. Why do politicians accept bribes? They are after things. Why do young hoodlums attack and even kill a teenage boy for his athletic shoes? They are after things. Why does a woman sell her body? She is after things. She wants to maintain a certain lifestyle. Why do businesses cut corners, cook the books, and pad their invoices? They are after things. Why does a drug dealer peddle his product to young kids and get them addicted? He is after things.

The lure of things is so powerful that even many Kingdom citizens who once were serious about their walk with God and their righteous positioning have been seduced by it. Once they could be seen at the church building every time the doors were open, at worship, at prayer meetings, at Bible study, participating in ministry projects. Now, however, they are almost never around. When you ask them why, they are always ready with an excuse: "Well, you know how it is. Times are tough. The economy is on the ropes and I've got to build my business. I don't have time for church right now. I've got to turn a profit. When I make a little more money, I'll come back and bless God with a portion." Or, "I have to work as much overtime as I can get. We just bought a new car and I have to make sure we can meet the payments." Or, "I had to take a second job because my regular job doesn't pay enough, and with my new job I have to work on Sundays."

On the surface these may sound like reasonable arguments, but in reality they take the exact opposite position to Jesus when He said, "*Seek first the Kingdom of God and His righteousness, and all these things will be added to you."* These folks have gotten things topsy-turvy. They have stopped seeking the Kingdom and righteousness and begun working for the things that should be added. And in so doing they move out of position and shut themselves off from access to the blessings, benefits, favor, protection, and promotion that belong by right to every Kingdom citizen. Remember, however, that the active, ongoing pursuit of righteousness is the key to access. Instead of honoring and obeying the God of all things, they have instead made things their god.

If only we would learn to take to heart the truth and wisdom of the ancient Hebrew proverb that says, *"The blessing of the Lord brings wealth, and He adds no trouble to it"* (Prov. 10:22)! Prosperity without pressure! Wealth without worry! Treasure without trouble! These are the realities when we live on Kingdom land and abide by the laws of the King who owns it all. Remember, the Kingdom contains everything that Kingdom citizens need. And all Kingdom citizens have access by right of citizenship to all the things of the Kingdom as long as they pursue the Kingdom and righteousness and not the things themselves. This is the cure for the dangerously seductive power of things.

THE ANSWER TO HUMAN MOTIVATION

Why is our human drive for things so strong? Because we believe that things will satisfy all our basic needs. As I pointed out in Chapter Two, there is little question that the meeting of needs is the ultimate motivation for all human behavior. The universal problem of humankind, however, is that in our efforts to meet our needs we expend all of our time, energy, and resources pursuing things that will never bring the satisfaction we seek. Why? Because we pursue the wrong things and look for satisfaction in the wrong places.

God designed us for life in His Kingdom and it is only there that we find satisfaction and fulfillment. The Kingdom of God is the ultimate response to our needs. It satisfies our longings and answers all our problems. Everything we humans seek is found in the Kingdom of God. *Everything*. Let me use this analogy: The Kingdom of God is the tree and the needs of people are the fruit. If you want the fruit you go to the tree.

Most people buy fruit at the grocery store or from a produce market. That's fine as long as the supply lasts. What happens if the supply line is cut or a shortage occurs? Suddenly, access to the fruit is cut off. If you want to ensure a steady supply of fruit, wouldn't it be better to own your own tree? That way fruit would be available whenever you wanted it.

In the world's system, the world is like the grocery store where we all must compete for limited resources. There is no competition in the Kingdom of God because its resources are unlimited. Every Kingdom citizen can have his or her own tree with an unfailing supply of fruit. When Jesus said, "Do not worry about what you will eat or drink or wear for clothing," He was asking, in effect, "Why run after the fruit and compete with everybody else when you can have the tree? Seek first the tree and all of the fruit will come with it."

In a similar analogy, the Kingdom of God is the *source* and "all these things" are the *resource*. Why spend all your time and energy chasing resources when Kingdom citizenship and righteousness will give you unhindered access to the Source? Never try to live for or depend on resources because resources run out. Get connected to God, the Source, because His resources never run out.

The pursuit of things never brings satisfaction because of one simple truth: *We don't need things to have life; we need life to have things.* Many people obsess over things because they derive their sense of personal worth and value from their possessions. They "need" a nice car in order to feel important. They must wear brand-name clothes to enhance their self-image. They must always buy the newest and latest thing if they are to feel fulfilled in life. Personal worth and importance are not found in these things, however. Self-worth and value are never found in things.

Our value and self-worth derive from who we are, not from what we have. We are of priceless worth to God irregardless of any possessions we own. Jesus used the example of the birds and how God feeds them even though they do not "*sow or reap or store away in barns*" (Matt. 6:26). He gives them the tree and the nest and the food simply because they are birds and need these things. The birds do not worry about it. They do not toil or sweat or chase after these things. They simply receive from the God who created them and who supplies everything they need to fulfill their purpose as birds. Then Jesus asks, "Are you not much more valuable than they?" In other words, if God supplies the birds' needs because they are birds, won't He also supply our needs because of who we are, human beings created in His image and much more valuable than birds?

Our innate importance attracts things. God does not give us things to make us important but because we *are* important. But we must never pursue things because that is the wrong focus. Instead we must pursue the Kingdom—our citizenship credentials—and righteousness, which is our right positioning with the Kingdom government. Then, when we are in the right position, God will provide everything He deems needful and appropriate for that position. This is the same idea as how earthly governments will provide their ambassadors with chauffeured limousines for official business rather than leaving them to putter around on motorbikes.

So the issue is not things, but living for the Kingdom. If all we care about is things, then we are on our own and must compete with the rest of the "pagans," but if we are serious about serving our Government, our King will add to us everything necessary to do so with grace and in a manner that reflects most favorably on His Kingdom. In other words, if we are serious about serving and representing the Kingdom of God with righteousness,

God will see to it that we are not forced to do so in a cheap or shabby manner.

God's intent was fulfillment without frustration. Jesus said, "*Seek first His kingdom and His righteousness, and all these things will be given to you as well*" (Matt. 6:33). Remember, as Lord of the universe, God owns everything. Nothing we have truly belongs to us and is not for us alone. When we seek His Kingdom and His righteousness, He gives us all these other things in order that we may fulfill our calling as Kingdom ambassadors and ministers of reconciliation.

Every human desires things. This is a God-given, and therefore godly, desire. What is ungodly is pursuing things as gods. God wants us to have them but He also wants to show us how to acquire them in the right way and with the proper spirit. He wants us to have plenty of things but He does not want us to pursue them at the expense of our relationship with Him. He knows that there are things we need and want but He does not want the desire for things to control our lives.

ACCESS IS A RIGHT OF CITIZENSHIP

The Kingdom of God contains everything its citizens need. And everything in the Kingdom belongs to the King. So access to the *things* of the Kingdom is a matter of belonging to the King. Once we belong to the King then everything that belongs to the King also belongs to us. By gaining the Kingdom we gain everything else.

Access to the things of the Kingdom is available to all Kingdom citizens by *right*. Rights are guaranteed by law. Citizens do not have to beg, plead, appease, or manipulate in order to receive what is theirs. In the event a citizen's legitimate rights are denied, either through error or malice, the citizen can petition the government in the court of law to have his or her rights restored and honored.

This is one of the main reasons why many born-again believers who are caught up in a religious mind-set do not see the benefits and prosperity and fruitfulness of the Kingdom manifesting in their lives. They approach the whole matter of Kingdom access as supplicants with pleas rather than as citizens with rights. Supplicants can be denied because they have no legal status. Their requests are at the mercy and benevolence of the governing authority. Citizens, on the other hand, are legal entities. Citizens have a legal claim on the activities of the government on their behalf. By constitutional law they are entitled to their rights and not even the government can legally deny them.

The average citizen in most countries is so ignorant of citizenship that the system runs their lives and they don't even know it. Many people live their entire lives effectively denied of rights they never knew they had. That is why it is so important for citizens to know their constitution, to understand how their government works, and to know what their rights are under the law. Many obstacles can be overcome simply by knowing—and asserting—your rights.

In 1980, in the early days of my ministry in the Bahamas, I decided, based on God's direction, to begin a radio ministry. I submitted a formal request to the appropriate governmental approval authority and indicated that I wished to broadcast during the day in the middle of the week. I was told that no religious broadcasting was allowed during the day. All religious programming was relegated to Sundays on the graveyard shift, which meant from 1 to 5 A.M. when no one would be awake except security people.

I persisted with my request, saying that I wanted to broadcast at 5 P.M. every Thursday so people who were in their cars heading home from work could listen. Once again I was told that it was not possible.

That's when I had a face-to-face meeting with the person in charge. As I sat across from him he said, "I'm sorry, Myles, but we can't do it."

"Let me start this over," I replied. "First, I am a citizen of this country. Second, I have broken no laws. Third, I have a product I wish to sell. Fourth, I have the right to do business in my community as long as I have not broken any laws. Fifth, you are here to serve me; I am not here to serve you."

Before it was all over, my request for a midweek radio broadcast ended up in Parliament. I was ready to take the government to court. Why? Because I was a citizen whose rights were being denied without good cause. I didn't appeal to a religion. I simply said, "I am a citizen and I have a right to do business. You cannot tell me when or where to sell my product."

In the end, the law was changed. Ours was the first ministry in the nation's history to broadcast a Christian program during the day in the middle of the week.

Several years later we went through the whole thing again when we prepared to launch a television ministry. Once again I had to stand up for my rights as a citizen. And once again our ministry was the first in the country to have a midweek television program.

In both of these circumstances I did not argue from a religious perspective. I did not beg or plead or cajole or manipulate anyone for anything. I appealed to my rights as a citizen. I went to the written code of law, the constitution.

Citizenship is powerful. It gives you access to all your rights under the law and even the government cannot deny you.

The Kingdom of God works the same way (except that, unlike many earthly governments, the King of Heaven is not hesitant or reluctant to honor the rights of His citizens). When you stand before God with the Kingdom constitution in your hand and say, "Thus says the constitution," the King will back you up because He stands behind His Word, His name, and His integrity. Access to the things of the Kingdom is a matter of knowing and claiming your rights. There is no begging involved.

Simply keep your pipeline clean—stay in position—and you can confidently expect everything the King has promised.

THE PURSUIT OF THINGS DISHONORS THE KING

It is wrong in a kingdom to pursue things because to do so dishonors the king. First of all, it is an expression of distrust toward the king. If you take charge of your own welfare in a kingdom by pursuing the things you need, you are saying that you do not trust the king to take care of his citizens. Remember a kingdom is different from a democracy. In a democracy you take care of yourself. The government provides the environment in which you can succeed, but basically you are on your own in securing the necessities, not to mention the niceties, of life. In a kingdom it is the reverse. Citizenship in a kingdom is imparted by the king, and once the king appoints citizens he immediately becomes obligated to sustain them.

In many ways it is like the parent-child relationship. Imagine your children coming to you every day with the same questions: "Are we going to have food today? Will we have something to drink today? Am I going to have good clothes to wear today?" As a parent you would be disappointed and probably hurt at your children's lack of faith in your ability and commitment to take care of them. Of course they will have food, drink, and clothing! You're their parent and you love them, and you also have a responsibility to care for them and provide for their needs. I think God feels the same way when He sees so many of us constantly fretting and sweating over our daily bread and other daily needs as if supplying those things was completely up to us.

As Kingdom citizens, we are sons and daughters of god. He is our heavenly Father and we are His royal princes and princesses. With that kind of relationship, how can we lose? The Father part means that He is obligated to take care of us, while the prince/princess part means that we have every right to expect it. We don't even have to think about it. So why worry?

The pursuit of things in a kingdom not only shows distrust but is also an insult to the king. It shows distrust by questioning the king's motives and intentions: "Does He really care about me? Will He take care of me?" It insults the king by questioning his ability: "Can He take care of me? Can He really provide what I need?" One of the keys to accessing the things of the Kingdom is coming to the place where we are completely confident that God possesses both the ability and the desire to supply everything we need.

One day when my son was still a little boy we were playing in the house. He was standing on the table and would run to the edge of the table and jump into my arms. I would catch him and then he would laugh. We did this several times. Then my wife called to me and I turned toward her just as he was running again. He jumped even though I had my back turned. I turned back around and caught him. Even when I had my back turned, my son still trusted me to catch him and not let him fall and get hurt. That's the kind of trust our heavenly Father is looking for from us, a childlike trust that never doubts that He will catch us and take care of us.

Some people would argue that this kind of trust is irresponsible. "What do you mean you're not worried about your mortgage payment or your car payment? Who's going to take care of them if you don't?" It's one thing to work conscientiously at your job to provide for your family; it's another thing to worry from day to day whether those needs will be met. Where do you draw the line between irresponsibility and trust? It depends on who you place your trust in. Trusting someone with an unreliable track record is irresponsible. Placing your faith in One who is completely and utterly faithful, on the other hand, is both responsible and sensible. You will never get very far in the Kingdom of God without the trust factor. There has to be a time when you realize that there is nothing holding you up except God, and if He fails, you have no "Plan B." Don't worry; with God covering you, there is no need for a "Plan B."

ACCESS TO THE THINGS OF THE KINGDOM REQUIRES THE CORRECT KEYS

The secret to accessing the things of the Kingdom of God is to have the right keys. Not literal keys, of course, but principles that open the floodgates of Heaven. Jesus told His disciples, *"I will give you the keys of the kingdom of Heaven"* (Matt. 16:19a), meaning the "access codes" or principles that would make Kingdom things operative in their lives.

Different keys open different locks. This is just as true in Heaven as it is on earth. Every nation has its own set of laws, legal principles under which it operates. Different laws apply to different circumstances and privileges. The laws that govern traffic are different than the laws that govern the courts. The laws that govern the medical institutions are different from the laws that govern the business institution. Each area of a country has different laws that regulate that area. If you obey the laws then you receive the privileges of the constitution. If you disobey the laws then those privileges are shut down.

Heaven is no different. Access to the things of Heaven requires the correct keys; knowledge and application of the correct principles that will release them. Possession of the keys to one area will not necessarily gain you access to another area. This is why on one occasion Jesus' disciples were unable to cast out a particular demon. Even though they had cast demons out earlier under Jesus' authority, on this occasion they failed. When the disciples asked Jesus why they had failed, He replied, *"This kind does not go out except by prayer and fasting"* (Matt. 17:21b). The disciples failed to cast out the demon because in that particular case they did not have the right keys, the keys of prayer and fasting.

In principle, gaining access to the things of Heaven is very simple: use the right key and you can open anything. The challenge comes in learning the nature of the different keys and where and how to apply them. This is very important because if you do not understand how the keys of the Kingdom work, you will become increasingly frustrated and depressed and possibly even come to the conclusion that what God said doesn't work. I was there at one point in my life and know how frightening it is.

Some of you may be there right now. You may be tithing, fasting, praying, and worshiping and yet nothing seems to be changing in your life. No matter how sincere you are, if you stand before a closed door with the wrong key, it will never open for you. Then it becomes easy to blame God because the door won't open. The problem is not with God or with the door. The problem is that you are using the wrong key.

So then what are the keys that give us access to the things of the Kingdom?

THE DIVINE OBLIGATION

Simply stated, the access keys to Kingdom things are the pursuit of the Kingdom of God and His righteousness. Seek these two things, Jesus said, and all the other things—the things of the Kingdom—would be added. But just what are "all these things"? What do they include? They cover every dimension of life. When your life is rightly aligned with God's government, "all these things" will be added to you:

- All your physical needs—food, drink, clothing, car, housing, health.

177

- All your social needs—all your relationships. God will add the right people in your
life.

- All your emotional needs—peace and a calm
and tranquil spirit for every situation. God
will deliver you from envy, jealousy, worry,
and vain striving and competition.

- All your psychological needs—stability. He
will give you the grace to avoid becoming
stressed out and burned out so you won't be
up one day and down the next. No matter
how your day or your week goes, good or
bad, you will be stable, knowing that God
will cause all things to work together for
your good (see Rom. 8:28).

- All your financial needs—wealth. This
includes both spiritual and material wealth,
both the tangible and the intangible, the visible and the invisible.

- All your security needs—protection. God
protects and overshadows the righteous. He
will never leave you or forsake you but will
always have His eyes fixed on you for your
good.

- All of your needs for self-significance—
value. God says, "I will give you back your
value. I will make you realize your inherent
importance once again. You are infinitely

valuable to me and I will restore your sense of self-worth."

- All your sense of purpose—vision. Instead of focusing on things you will once more focus on your assignment and move toward your destiny. You will stop living to make a living and start living to make a difference.

All these things will be added to you when you apply the keys of a whole-hearted seeking of the Kingdom and righteousness of God. What a way to live!

All these things will be freely given to you by the King of things, Jesus Christ Himself, of whom it is written: *"Through Him all things were made; without Him nothing was made that has been made"* (John 1:3), and, *"His divine power has given us everything we need for life and godliness through our knowledge of Him who called us by His own glory and goodness"* (2 Pet. 1:3).

The secret key to Kingdom things is position and disposition. Disposition is Kingdom citizenship. Position is righteousness. Position and disposition: those are the keys. Get your citizenship in order and then stay in right relationship with the heavenly country and all these things will be added to you.

Things are not blessings. They are by-products of Kingdom citizenship. That is why the all-consuming pursuit of things is out of order. It is like putting the cart before the horse. Seek first the Kingdom and righteousness of God. Get your citizenship credentials in order and the things will come—everything you need, without exception.

PRINCIPLES

1. Pursuit of things is always the wrong focus.

2. The active, ongoing pursuit of righteousness is the key to access.

3. The Kingdom of God is the ultimate response to humankind's needs.

4. We don't need things to have life; we need life to have things.

5. Our value and self-worth derive from who we are, not from what we have.

6. God does not give us things to make us important but because we are important.

7. The issue is not things, but living for the Kingdom.

8. God's intent was fulfillment without frustration.

9. Access to the things of the Kingdom is available to all Kingdom citizens by right.

10. The access keys to Kingdom things are the pursuit of the Kingdom of God and His righteousness.

11. The secret key to Kingdom things is position and disposition. Disposition is Kingdom citizenship. Position is righteousness.

12. Things are not blessings. They are by-products of Kingdom citizenship.

"Hard work can make you a living, but submission to principles adds to your life."

CHAPTER NINE

THE KINGDOM
PRINCIPLE OF ADDITION

S ome time ago while boarding an airplane I happened to catch one of the flight attendants in a
yawn. (I'm glad it wasn't the pilot!) "Good after-
noon," I said to her. "How are you doing today?"

"I'm tired," she answered.

"Why are you tired?"

"I have two jobs."

"Why do you need two jobs?" I asked.

She replied, "I have to pay my bills. I like the finer
things of life."

"So, you're sleepy?"

"Yes," she said. "I go right from this job to my other
job."

"So when do you sleep?"

"Oh, every once in awhile," she answered. "Whenever
I can."

Here was a person who was always running after
things. Why? Because she liked "the finer things of life."

Between working two jobs and trying to grab sleep whenever possible, when did she have time to enjoy them? This flight attendant was a young woman but she already looked old, tired, and worn out. Her ceaseless pursuit of things was aging her prematurely.

Sadly, she's not alone. Most of the people in our modern, consumer-driven culture are in the same situation. Because of their unremitting obsession with things they are perpetually tired, distracted, depressed, irritable and, if not sick already, prime candidates for stress- and anxiety-induced illness. The pursuit of things is detrimental to our health.

Jesus said it was never meant to be this way. He said that we are not supposed to work for food or water or clothing or any of the other things we need on a regular basis. Those things are supposed to come to us in the natural course of living our lives according to God's design and intention. The reason they do not is because we do not understand the Kingdom of God or how it works. Dispelling that misunderstanding and demonstrating how to find fulfillment without frustration is the purpose of this book.

We must understand the Kingdom of God in order to avoid the mistake of seeking it merely for its benefits. The Kingdom is not a tool for us to use to get things from God. That is not the purpose of the Kingdom. Sometimes we treat faith as if it were a lottery, that if we play it just right we will win the big jackpot. It is easy to abuse the Kingdom *message* the same way. Blessings and provision are a real, natural, and vital part of Kingdom life, but if we are not careful we will end up making them the object of our faith rather than its natural by-product.

Throughout this book I have told about how "all these things" will be *added* to those who seek first the Kingdom and righteousness of God. We can call this the *Kingdom Principle of Addition*. It is appropriate now to examine this principle of addition in greater depth. In doing so, we will better understand the King's plan for His citizens' provision.

THE TWO PRIORITIES OF GOD

As mentioned previously, when Jesus came preaching the gospel of the Kingdom of Heaven, He neatly reduced all the issues, concerns, and strivings of humankind into two simple but profound priorities: (1) to seek the Kingdom of God and (2) to seek the righteousness of God. These two priorities are all-important; everything else is secondary. With that simple message Jesus destroyed every reason most of us have for going to work. He stripped away the very things that motivate us to get out of bed in the morning. Instead of working to live we are supposed to work for the Kingdom. Instead of living for work we are supposed to live for righteousness. If we do these things, Jesus promised, God will add everything else to us. They will come to us without our having to work or worry over them.

This is the Kingdom way of thinking and living. Yet, we are so thoroughly programmed to concern ourselves every day with our own provision that it is hard to learn to think another way. God wants to supply our needs, but as long as we insist on taking charge of it ourselves, we tie His hands. To put it another way, as long as we insist on doing it ourselves, we will never open the door to the abundant things of the Kingdom of Heaven. Self-sufficiency and self-effort are the wrong keys. As we saw in the previous chapter, disposition (Kingdom citizenship) and position (righteousness) are the keys that will open that door. If you want the Kingdom principle of addition to work for you, make sure first of all that you have become a Kingdom citizen through the new birth by faith in Christ and, second of all, that you are living in alignment with Kingdom law. If those two things are in place, the King will add everything else to your life.

The Kingdom principle of addition operates on obedience: faithful observance of Kingdom law and clean living. These are the same standards God has always required of His people. Consider these words that Moses spoke to the ancient Israelites:

> *You will again obey the Lord and follow all His commands I am giving you today. Then the Lord your God will make you most prosperous in all the work of your hands and in the fruit of your womb, the young of your livestock and the crops of your land. The Lord will again delight in you and make you prosperous, just as He delighted in your fathers, if you obey the Lord your God and keep His commands and decrees that are written in this Book of the Law and turn to*

the Lord your God with all your heart and with all your soul (Deuteronomy 30:8-10).

The Israelites were east of the Jordan River, ready to cross over and take possession of Canaan, the land God had promised to them as far back as Abraham. They have spent the last 40 years as nomads in the desert, during which time the oldest generation of them, those who were already adults when they left Egypt, have died off due to their rebellion against God. Now God is renewing His promise to this new generation, which is why Moses said, "You will *again* obey the Lord," and "The Lord will *again* delight in you." God's renewed promise is to make them prosperous in everything they do: in their work, family life, and in their harvests. In short, God promises to provide for them in every way. His stipulation: that they obey His commands and love Him whole-heartedly.

The same stipulation applies to us today. We cannot expect God to add things to us if we are living in sin. That is why many of us fret and sweat just to pay our bills every month. We're not living right. Our lives are out of alignment with God's government. The rewards of the Kingdom on God's part require right living on our part.

Worship alone is not enough. Neither is praying. Right living means making a deliberate, clean break with sin, accompanied by confession if necessary, and a resolute, careful determination to live every day in obedience to the laws of God. It means laying aside dishonesty, immorality, coarse or foul language, gossip, slander, backbiting, backstabbing, envy, jealousy, pride, selfish ambition, and lying. Right living means taking up a humble spirit of submission and service to God in which we first love God with all our heart and then love our neighbor as ourselves.

THE DIVINE STRATEGY FOR PROVISION

In order to unlock God's divine strategy for provision, we must first somehow break out of our traditional mind-set that says that unless we sweat and labor and strive and concentrate all our energy on our daily needs, they will not be met. Maybe that's the way you feel. Perhaps you are struggling with this whole idea of seeking first the Kingdom and righteousness of God and leaving everything else to Him. All this does not mean that you don't work to support your family; it means that you don't obsess over meeting your needs. Instead, you seek to obey God in your daily life and trust Him to provide as He has promised.

God wants to pay your bills. He knows you need food and water and shelter. He wants you to have a nice house that is suitable for your family. He wants you to have a car. He wants you to have a bike. God wants to give you the desires of your heart. As a matter of fact, He wants to fulfill your highest dreams because He is the one who put those dreams in your heart. What He does not want is for you to put your dreams and desires ahead of Him. That's why Jesus says that all these things will be *added* to you.

But what exactly does "added" mean? When God adds to your life it means:

1. Things will be attracted to you. They will be added like a magnet.

2. Things will find you. You won't have to chase them or hunt them down.

3. Things will come to your life. They may appear suddenly and unexpectedly and often from an unexpected source or direction.

4. Things will come without stress. Some people are so tired from working for what they want that when they finally get it they are too stressed out to enjoy it. That's nothing but foolishness. Life is to be savored and enjoyed, not stressed over. When God adds to your life He will add it without stress.

5. Things will be given as a favor and reward, like a gift, not as something you earned.

6. Things will come without struggle. You won't have to fight or compete or play "keep up with the Joneses." When it comes, it will be effortless on your part.

7. Things will be seen as natural. When something is added to your life it will come naturally, as if it was inevitable.

8. Things will be given to you as needed. Remember, God adds things not for your personal benefit or selfish use alone but for fulfilling His purpose. If you don't really need something, don't be surprised if you do not receive it until you do need it.

9. Things will not be pursued. If you are pursuing the Kingdom and righteousness, you won't have time to pursue other things as your highest priority. That's why God will give them to you.

10. Things will not be your source. Things are commodities, tools, resources to be used to advance God's Kingdom on earth. Don't look to them as your source of happiness or self-worth or fulfillment. God is your source. Look to Him.

THE ADDITION PRINCIPLE

The Kingdom principle of addition is founded on four significant truths that are uniquely characteristic of kingdoms. All four relate to the relationship that exists between the King and His citizens.

1. *All that is needed for sustenance and life is the obligation of the king.*

In a democracy, every citizen has to earn his own living and make his own way. The government tries to create an environment in which every citizen can succeed but takes no direct responsibility for the care and welfare of its citizens at a personal level. Success levels among citizens vary due to education, motivation, opportunity, and a host of other factors. This is why every democratic society has rich people, poor people, and those in between.

Compare this to a kingdom, where the care and welfare of every citizen is the direct and personal responsibility of the king. This doesn't mean, of course, that the king personally visits every citizen and takes care of every need single-handedly—a wise king delegates those responsibilities—but it does mean that the buck stops with him. Anything that any citizen lacks reflects poorly on the king and on the quality of his rule. A king, therefore, has a vested interest in making sure all his citizens prosper, because prosperous citizens make for a prosperous kingdom. And a prosperous kingdom brings glory to the king. In fact, a king is obligated to take care of his citizens because he owns everything in his kingdom and they will have nothing unless he gives it to them. Consequently, and unlike a democracy, there are no poor people in a kingdom. Nobody is poor because nobody owns anything. But all citizens have equal access to the king's assets.

I am speaking, of course, of an *ideal* kingdom, a *perfect* kingdom with a perfect, omnipotent and benevolent king who always and in every situation works for the good and greater welfare of his citizens. Clearly, no such kingdom can be found among today's earthly governments. Only the Kingdom of Heaven and its divine King meet these criteria. And He has promised to meet the needs and protect the welfare of His people.

2. *Provisions for life are the responsibility of the king and not the citizen.*

Democracies are built on the principles of capitalism and free and open markets. Every person in a democracy is free to make his or her own way, free to seek and enjoy the good life. In fact, they are obligated to because no one will do it for them. Yet for many, including many believers, making their own way isn't working. The daily rat race really drags them down. Every day is a struggle, money is always in short supply, and they see no end in sight to these circumstances. Common wisdom says, "Go for your piece of the pie," but the pie is so small that there seems not to be enough for everybody to get some. Consequently, most people live and die never having tasted anything but crumbs.

This is the system we live in on earth, but Jesus says, "That's all wrong! You are Kingdom citizens. Provision for life is not your responsibility; it's mine. So stop worrying about all this stuff. Let Me take care of it! I know it's tough to break away from the system because the system is built for dependency. Nevertheless, let go of the system. Learn to depend on Me."

Some of you may wonder if I am advising you to become irresponsible. Not at all. I'm actually encouraging you to become more responsible by trusting the

King. It takes more responsibility to live in the Kingdom than to live in the system of the world.

3. *Kingdom favor is the unearned provision of the king.*

The Kingdom of Heaven does not operate on a system of wages and earnings. This is a good thing, because none of us could ever earn our way into Heaven. Eternal life is unavailable to us, completely out of our reach, unless it is given (added) to us as a gift. And this is exactly what God has done: *"For the wages of sin is death, but the gift of God is eternal life in Christ Jesus our Lord"* (Rom. 6:23).

The gift of God's unearned provision is called *favor.* He gives because He chooses to, not because we deserve it. Favor is the system upon which the Kingdom of Heaven operates. Nothing we receive in the Kingdom do we receive because we worked for it. Anything we work for constitutes earnings, not additions. Additions always come to us unearned.

Yet still we work and fret and labor and sweat to secure the things we need and want and wonder why the Kingdom of Heaven is not "working" for us. The answer is very simple: *the Kingdom does not operate on works; it operates on favor.* We cannot expect the Kingdom's provisions to come our way until we learn to operate by the Kingdom's system.

4. *Man was never designed to pursue personal provisions but the influence of Heaven on earth.*

Our purpose on earth as Kingdom citizens and ambassadors is to spread the awareness and the influence of God's Kingdom throughout the earth. Pursuing provision was never part of God's master plan for us. That's why Jesus said, "Don't worry about food or drink or clothing, because your heavenly Father knows you need these things." When we are about our Kingdom purpose, our King will supply all the provisions we need to do the job.

The "Lord's Prayer" (or "Model Prayer") recorded in Matthew 6:9-13, which Jesus used to teach His disciples how to pray, contains only one phrase related to provision: *"Give us today our daily bread"* (Matt. 6:11). This phrase serves to reorient our hearts and minds to the One who is our true Source and Provider. The real focus of our prayers should be, *"Our Father in Heaven, hallowed be Your name, Your Kingdom come, Your will be done on earth as it is in Heaven"* (Matt. 6:9-10). In other words, we should pray (and work) for the influence of the Kingdom to advance throughout the earth and let the King handle all the logistics. God's desire is that we not live for things, but live for His influence.

KINGDOM PROVISION AND PURPOSE

Provision is a by-product of obedience. It is not a wage paid for work performed or for services rendered. Jesus promised that if we seek the Kingdom and righteousness of God that all the provisions we need for life will be added to us. Everything necessary for us to live righteously as Kingdom citizens will be provided. But our heart and mind, our will and desire, must be inclined toward consistent obedience to the King.

This kind of obedience involves much more than simple adherence to external rules and regulations or mere outward behavioral changes. You can obey on the outside and still possess a rebellious, disobedient heart. This is a very old problem, extending as far back as the Garden of Eden. In fact, the ancient Hebrew prophet Isaiah records this complaint of God about His people: *"The Lord says: 'These people come near to me with their mouth and honor me with their lips, but their hearts are far from me. Their worship of me is made up only of rules taught by men'"* (Isa. 29:13). As far as God is concerned, external obedience with a disobedient heart is not obedience at all.

Obedience that releases Kingdom provision begins in the heart and manifests in our outward lives. In other words, true external obedience is the result of an obedient heart. False external obedience is nothing more than a calculated ploy to manipulate God into giving us what we want, and it will fail every time. This is why many believers are perplexed today. They go to church, they read their Bible, they pray, they give their tithe and their time, and yet nothing seems to be working. The Kingdom storehouse is still shut to them. The reason? They are not living right. Their hearts are not clean and pure before God. Despite their outward display of righteousness, their hearts are out of alignment with the Kingdom government.

In the Bible, abundant provision and prosperity clearly are linked to obedience to God. Shortly before the Israelites crossed the Jordan River into the Promised Land, Moses gave then this charge and promise from God:

> *Now it shall come to pass, if you diligently obey the voice of the Lord your God, to observe carefully all His commandments which I command you today, that the Lord your God will set you high above all nations of the earth. And all these blessings shall come upon you and overtake you, because you obey the voice of the Lord your God: "Blessed shall you be in the city, and blessed shall you be in the country. Blessed shall be the fruit of your body, the produce of your ground and the increase of your herds, the increase of your cattle and the offspring of your flocks. Blessed shall be your basket and your kneading bowl. Blessed shall you be when you come in, and blessed shall you be when you go out"* (Deuteronomy 28:1-6 NKJV).

When we obey the Lord with our whole heart, His blessings will "overtake" us. This means that when God's blessings come to us, they will be more than we know what to do with. To be blessed in the fruit of our body and the produce of our ground means that God will bless and guard our investments. The increase in our herds means that the accumulations of our wealth will be multiplied.

Everywhere we go, wherever we turn and in whatever we touch we will be blessed. Success, favor, and influence for the Kingdom will expand at every turn.

If we obey God's commands from our heart, the provisions of the Kingdom will overtake us.

In addition to the issue of obedience in the Kingdom, is the issue of ownership. *The principle of provision and prosperity in the Kingdom is access, not ownership or pursuit.* Wealth in the Kingdom of God is defined not as having things stored up but rather having access to things that are stored up. When we avidly and anxiously pursue things such as food, water, clothing, housing, and the like, we imply that we believe these things are scarce, and unless we fight alongside everybody else we will not get our piece of the pie.

There is no lack of anything in the Kingdom of God; no shortages and no rationing. On the contrary, there are boundless amounts of everything. The King owns everything; we own nothing. Because the King owns everything, He can give anything in any amount to any of His children anytime He wants to. The principle of provision and addition involves being in the position through right living to have access to as much as we need of anything that we need to carry out our assignment from God.

Look at it this way. Imagine that your father is a billionaire and he says to you, "I will give you a choice. I will either set up a $1 million account for you to live on that is exclusively yours or, in lieu of your own account, I will give you complete and unlimited access to everything I have." Which would you choose: $1 million that is yours free and clear or free access to billions? It's a no-brainer! And yet when it comes to matters of the Kingdom of God, many of us pass on unlimited access in favor of getting and hoarding our little piece of the pie. Does that make any sense? True wealth is found not in an abundance of possessions but in unlimited access to infinite resources.

We need access to such resources because *man was not created to work for provision but for purpose.* And what is our purpose? To spread the knowledge and influence of the Kingdom of Heaven over all the earth. Success in such an assignment requires adequate daily provision. Just as no wise general will send his troops onto the battlefield without making sure they have all the equipment and provisions they need to accomplish their mission, neither will God send us forth to fulfill our purpose without providing us with the resources to carry it out. So whenever and wherever we go to work we should be motivated not by the promise of a paycheck but by the calling of our King to spread His Kingdom throughout the world, starting in our own workplace.

Man was created to work out his assignment, not work for a living. This doesn't mean we stop working; it means we change our reason for working. Working for a paycheck can inspire only so far and for only so long. But to go to work every day knowing that we are living for a higher purpose—an eternal purpose—can place our work in a whole new light.

In the Kingdom, assignment determines access. What does that mean? It's very simple. Whatever you were born to do is how rich you are. If you are trying to get rich so you can say you are richer than everybody else, your pursuit will end up killing you (or make you so miserable you will wish you were dead). If you are committed to your Kingdom purpose, however, God will prosper you to whatever degree necessary for you to succeed. In the Kingdom of God, your assignment determines your access to the provisions of the King.

It is far more important to find our assignment than to pursue things because the things that come into our lives come to help us fulfill our God-given assignment. If God has given you a $10 billion assignment, pursue that assignment faithfully and He will give you the $10 billion. We do not receive wealth for ourselves but for carrying out our assignment. That's why Jesus told us not to worry about things. Pursue the Kingdom assignment first and the things will be added.

Therefore, *in the Kingdom, purpose attracts provision.* Whenever a king makes an assignment, he makes full provision for its completion. When Nehemiah received permission from the king of Persia to return to Jerusalem and rebuild its walls, the king gave him a letter authorizing him to utilize whatever of the king's resources were necessary, whether wood from the king's forests or stone from the king's quarries or tar from the king's tar pits. Nehemiah embarked on his task confident that he had everything he needed to succeed.

The King of Heaven is the same way. God will never assign us something that He does not give us the provisions to complete. Our part is to pursue the end—the assignment; God's part is to supply the means. This is why establishing our priorities is so important. Priority with purpose produces provision.

PROVISION IS TIED TO PURPOSE

When Jesus wanted to explain to His followers the proper attitude they should take toward provision and the pursuit of things, He chose an example from nature:

> *Therefore I tell you, do not worry about your life, what you will eat or drink, or about your body, what you will wear. Is not life more important than food , and the body more important than clothes? Look at the birds of the air; they do not sow or reap or store away in barns, and yet your heavenly Father feeds them. Are you not much more valuable than they? Who of you by worrying can add a single hour to his life?* (Matthew 6:25-27)

After encouraging His followers not to worry about daily needs, Jesus then said that life is more than working for food and other necessities. If all we live for is the next paycheck and making ends meet, then we are missing out on life. He also said that the body is more than just a display rack for fancy clothes. In effect, Jesus is saying to us, "Your body really wasn't made to wear clothes. I created your body so that I could come into the earth through you and establish My Kingdom on earth. I want to fulfill an assignment through you, and the clothing you wear is completely immaterial except as they relate to that assignment."

To drive home the point that it is needless to worry, Jesus directs their attention to the birds. Birds do not sow seed, they do not reap a harvest and they do not store up food in a barn, and yet they never go hungry because God feeds them. First, they do not sow. In other words, birds do not work to live. They live to be birds. Second, they do not reap. Birds do not collect a paycheck. They don't need to because God has already given them everything they need to fulfill their purpose of being birds. Third, they do not store up. Birds do not hoard. They do not become obsessed or stressed out over making sure they have enough for tomorrow or next week or next year. They simply take what they receive each day and are perfectly content. Have you ever heard of a bird with heart trouble or high blood pressure or cancer? I haven't.

A bird doesn't try to be a horse. It doesn't try to be a fish or a monkey or a human. A bird simply preoccupies itself with being a bird. It has no desire to be anything else. It is perfectly content to fulfill its purpose as a bird. God created the bird to be that way and He gives the bird everything it needs to be a bird. God created the tree in which the bird builds its nest. He provided the twigs the bird gathers to put in the nest as well as the cotton plants from which the bird collects padding for its nest. God made the leaves for shading the nest. And He made the wind that enables the bird to fly to its nest and lay its eggs.

The bird has everything it needs to be a perfect bird, and God takes care of it. However, if you climbed onto the roof of your house and jumped off in an effort to fly, you would immediately regret your decision! If the fall didn't kill you, your stay in the hospital would provide you ample time to reconsider your actions. Why couldn't you fly like a bird? Because flying is not your purpose. God's promise to add "all these things" does not include things to make you bird-like. Provision is tied to purpose. Just as God gives the birds everything they need to be birds, He will give us everything we need to fulfill our purpose as Kingdom citizens and royal children of the King.

When we set out to seek the Kingdom and righteousness of God, we don't need to concern ourselves about provisions for the journey because the provisions come with the territory. All we have to do is work at being a Kingdom ambassador, and everything we need for executing that office will be provided for us.

PRINCIPLES

1. The Kingdom principle of addition operates on obedience—faithful observance of Kingdom law and clean living.

2. The rewards of the Kingdom on God's part require right living on our part.

3. In a kingdom, the care and welfare of every citizen is the direct and personal responsibility of the king.

4. All citizens have equal access to the king's assets.

5. The Kingdom does not operate on works; it operates on favor.

6. When we are about our Kingdom purpose, our King will supply all the provisions we need to do the job.

7. God's desire is that we not live for things but live for His influence.

8. Provision is a by-product of obedience.

9. When we obey the Lord with our whole heart, His blessings will "overtake" us.

10. The principle of provision and prosperity in the Kingdom is access, not ownership or pursuit.

11. True wealth is found not in an abundance of possessions, but in unlimited access to infinite resources.

12. In the Kingdom, assignment determines access.

13. Our part is to pursue the end—the assignment. God's part is to supply the means.

14. Provision is tied to purpose.

*"A stingy man with much wealth
is a danger to a world of poor men."*

Chapter Ten

SERVICE: THE HEART OF KINGDOM CULTURE

From the beginning, God's original purpose and plan was to rule the earth from Heaven through His family of humankind. He created man for this very reason. Man's original purpose was to dominate the earth through Kingdom influence. God's strategy for accomplishing this was to establish a colony of Heaven on earth. His intention was to influence the earth from Heaven so that the earth would begin to take on the culture of Heaven. In this manner, the influence of the invisible heavenly Kingdom would permeate, fill, and cover the visible physical earthly realm.

A kingdom, as we have already seen, is the governing influence of a king over his territory, impacting it with his will, his intent and his purpose, manifesting that impact through the development of a culture that is manifested in its citizens. In other words, every kingdom manifests itself in the lifestyle and culture of its people. This means that every citizen of a kingdom is supposed to take on the nature of the king. That is why, for example, we speak British English in the Bahamas. We call it the "King's English" because our lifestyle and culture reflect the influence of the British crown.

God's intent for us as Kingdom citizens is that we take on the culture of Heaven so that in whatever we do or say it will be evident that we belong to the Kingdom of Heaven. That is why we don't use foul language or lie or cheat or practice deceit or give way to jealousy or hatred. Those things are not part of Heaven's culture and therefore are foreign to us. As Kingdom citizens we are from God's country and both our language and our lifestyle should reflect that.

Remember, the Kingdom of God is not a religion. It is an actual country with its own government, laws, culture, and citizenry. And unlike earthly kingdoms of men, the Kingdom of Heaven is an eternal Kingdom. The Old Testament prophet Daniel said of God, *"How great are His signs, how mighty His wonders! His kingdom is an eternal kingdom; His dominion endures from generation to generation"* (Dan. 4:3). Even the oldest nations on earth have been organized states for less than 2,000 years. That may be a long time from man's perspective but it is merely a drop in the bucket compared to eternity. An eternal Kingdom needs to be taken seriously. The Kingdom of Heaven will still be around after every kingdom of man has fallen to dust.

God's Kingdom will endure from generation to generation. This means that there is a place in the Kingdom not only for us but also for our children, grandchildren, great-grandchildren, and all other generations of our descendents until the end of time. If the Kingdom dies with us as far as our family is concerned, then we will have failed our King. God is always looking for more citizens for His Kingdom, and if we fail in our generation, who will introduce future generations to the Kingdom?

The Kingdom of Heaven is our inheritance. Again, from the words of Daniel, *"The saints of the Most High will receive the kingdom and will possess it forever—yes, for ever and ever"* (Dan. 7:18). *Saints* is another word for Kingdom citizens. We are destined to possess the Kingdom that Jesus Christ came to earth to announce and establish.

As I have mentioned before, Christ did not bring a religion but a Kingdom, a royal government. Christianity is a religion, which is why it doesn't work. You can practice a religion but you can't practice citizenship. This is why some folks are good on Sunday and a mess on Monday. They're practicing religion. But you can't practice citizenship. Being a Kingdom citizen is a 24-hour-a-day reality, which is just what God wants. He doesn't want members, but citizens. He wants people on earth who are citizens of a country from another place. That is why as Kingdom citizens we are in the world but not of the world.

In bringing the Kingdom of Heaven to earth, Christ was restoring what man lost in the Garden of Eden. Yet somewhere along the way we missed the point and substituted a religion for the Kingdom. Jesus said, *"Blessed are the poor in spirit, for theirs is the kingdom of Heaven"*

(Matt. 5:3). "Poor in spirit" means spiritually bankrupt, spiritually destitute and in great spiritual need. Jesus said that the Kingdom of Heaven is reserved for those who recognize their spiritual poverty. If you are spiritually empty, no religion, including institutionalized, man-centered Christianity, can fill your emptiness. You will never be satisfied until you receive the Kingdom.

This is why Jesus was so insistent that we seek *first* the Kingdom and righteousness of God and trust Him to provide all the things that we need for daily life. The enemy likes nothing more than to distract us into pursuing things because it keeps our attention away from the Kingdom and our Kingdom destiny.

THE KINGDOM OF HEAVEN HAS A DISTINCTIVE CULTURE

Jesus always talked about the Kingdom. It was His only message. One time He said, *"The kingdom of Heaven is like yeast that a woman took and mixed into a large amount of flour until it worked all through the dough"* (Matt. 13:33). This parable is a statement about Kingdom influence. One thing about yeast, once you add it to your dough you cannot remove it. It's there for good. And although it works slowly at first, eventually the yeast permeates the entire batch of dough.

In the same way, now that the Kingdom of Heaven is on earth, it will never depart. And like yeast, the Kingdom is growing and will continue to grow until it thoroughly covers and saturates the earth. Although human governments come and go, the government of God will last forever. His Kingdom is eternal.

The presence of the Kingdom of Heaven on earth divides all the people on earth into two groups: those who are Kingdom citizens and those who are not. This is a critical distinction. Our purpose as Kingdom citizens is to work with the King to increase the size of the first group and decrease the size of the second group. We have a calling and a responsibility to influence earthly culture with the culture of Heaven. For this very reason, the King has given us Kingdom authority—the keys of the Kingdom—so that we can fulfill our calling as ministers of reconciliation.

Every country has a culture. Culture is the manifestation of the nature of the government in the lifestyle, customs, and morals of the people. In other words, every country has unique qualities of character, customs, traditions, and social mores that distinguish it from other countries. In practical terms this means that when you enter the Kingdom of Heaven through the new birth in Christ, you become a Kingdom citizen and the culture of the Kingdom should begin to manifest in your life, your speech, and your behavior.

When you return to work, your boss and your co-workers should notice such a difference in your manner and behavior that it will prompt them to ask you what has changed about you. That is when you can say, "Yes, something is different. I have changed countries and am now a citizen of a different government. I am in this world but not of it. My citizenship is from another place."

Kingdom culture is distinctly different from the cultures of any earthly country. The Kingdom operates under different principles and laws than those of the world and thus produces a distinctive culture that stands out in the world. One of the clearest distinctives of Kingdom culture is that it is a culture characterized by service. The cultures of the world manifest an every-man-for-himself approach to life and success. Kingdom culture, however, measures success by service and self-giving. Kingdom culture is a culture of servanthood.

A CULTURE OF SERVANTHOOD

Jesus modeled consistently in word and deed the character quality of servanthood. He also taught it as a fundamental principle of Kingdom life. One of His most explicit teachings on the subject came in response to a request he received from the mother of James and John, two of His closest disciples.

Then the mother of Zebedee's sons came to Jesus with her sons and, kneeling down, asked a favor of him.

"What is it you want?" he asked.

She said, "Grant that one of these two sons of mine may sit at your right and the other at your left in your kingdom."

"You don't know what you are asking," Jesus said to them." Can you drink the cup I am going to drink?"

"We can," they answered.

Jesus said to them, "You will indeed drink from My cup, but to sit at my right or left is not for Me to grant. These places belong to those for whom they have been prepared by My Father" (Matthew 20:20-23).

This woman was like all loving mothers; she wanted the best for her boys. She wanted them to be great men, men of authority in the Kingdom that Jesus was establishing. She hoped to persuade Jesus to promote her sons to positions of greatness and power. Her problem lay in the fact that she approached the matter from the attitude and value system of the world. She did not yet understand the dynamics of the Kingdom. She did not understand that the values, standards, principles, and priorities of the Kingdom were very different from those in the world.

Jesus' response was less than she (and her sons) had hoped. He said that the positions on either side of Him in the Kingdom were not His to give. Those choices were for His Father to make.

Understandably, Jesus' other disciples were upset over all of this, which gave Jesus the opportunity to teach them all about greatness from the Kingdom perspective.

When the ten heard about this, they were indignant with the two brothers. Jesus called them together and said, "You know that the rulers of the Gentiles lord it over them, and their high officials exercise authority over them. Not so with you. Instead, whoever wants to become great among you must be your servant, and whoever wants to be first must be your slave— just as the Son of Man did not come to be served but to serve, and to give his life as a ransom for many" (Matthew 20:24-28).

Jesus said that in the Kingdom, you don't find greatness by seeking titles or position. Greatness in the Kingdom does not come by advancing over your co-workers and then lording your elevation over them. In the Kingdom, you serve your way to greatness. You don't connive your way to greatness. The mother of James and John sought greatness for her sons by association instead of dedication. She hoped to exploit her sons' "inner track" to Jesus for their advantage. After all, that is how the world operates. You get ahead according to who you know.

But Jesus nipped that idea in the bud. He said, "In My Kingdom you don't achieve greatness by who you associate with but rather by how well you serve others." His own life was the perfect example. Jesus, even though He was the Son of God, came to serve, not to be served. What was appropriate for Him is certainly appropriate for us. The road to greatness in the Kingdom of Heaven leads through the valley of humble service.

Jesus said, "Whoever wants to become great among you must be your servant, and whoever wants to be *first* must be your slave." In this context, the word *first* means the first one people always call on. In other words, the one who is the most important, the one who is most valuable, the one who everyone calls first is the one with the reputation for working the hardest.

If people are always calling on you or turning to you, that's a good sign. However, if you are the one they always avoid, perhaps it is time for you to reexamine your attitude, habits, and work ethic. No one ever becomes great by avoiding the hard jobs and the tough decisions. And if you do not have the spirit of service and hard work, it will not be only people avoiding you. Prosperity will avoid you as well.

Being a servant does not mean that you become subservient. It means that you find what you have and you give it to the world. You serve your gift to the world. That's what makes you great in the Kingdom of Heaven.

THE LIFE OF A SHEEP

The Kingdom of Heaven is our inheritance. It is our past as well as our future. And the principle of humble service plays a central role to our entering in. Jesus told of the day at the end of time when He will sit on His throne of glory with all the nations gathered before Him for judgment. There will be only two groups of people: the "sheep," or the righteous, at His right hand, and the "goats," or the unrighteous, at His left.

Then the King will say to those on His right, "Come, you who are blessed by My Father; take your inheritance, the kingdom prepared for you since the creation of the world. For I was hungry and you gave

215

Me something to eat, I was thirsty and you gave Me
something to drink, I was a stranger and you invited
Me in. I needed clothes and you clothed Me, I was
sick and you looked after Me, I was in prison and
you came to visit Me" (Matthew 25:34-36).

Notice that the inheritance of the righteous is not
Heaven but the Kingdom of Heaven. Remember that the
Kingdom of Heaven is a country with a government and
influence on the earth. It is yeast that is making its way
through the minds and cultures of humankind. The
Kingdom is not new but has existed since creation, waiting to be populated by the righteous. The time has come,
and Jesus says to them, "Come, take your inheritance."

Then Jesus describes the character of the righteous
that sets them apart from the unrighteous, the character
of service and a servant heart. It is practical service: feeding the hungry, giving drink to the thirsty, welcoming the
stranger, clothing the naked, tending the sick, and visiting
the imprisoned. Notice also that Jesus views all of these
actions of compassion as being performed for Him: "I
was hungry...I was thirsty...I was a stranger...I needed
clothes...I was sick...I was in prison."

Characteristically, the righteous servants respond
with humility (not false modesty):

Then the righteous will answer Him, "Lord, when did
we see You hungry and feed You, or thirsty and give
You something to drink? When did we see You a
stranger and invite You in, or needing clothes and

SERVICE: THE HEART OF KINGDOM CULTURE

clothe You? When did we see you sick or in prison and go to visit You?"

The King will reply, "I tell you the truth, whatever you did for one of the least of these brothers of mine, you did for Me" (Matthew 25:37-40).

Humble service is so natural and so second nature to those with a servant heart that they do not think of themselves as having done anything special or of particular merit. If asked about their actions they would say, "It is the least I could do." True servants have no ulterior motives. They are not out to get noticed nor do they seek to use their service as a steppingstone to some greater or higher position. True servants live to serve and are delighted to do so.

Jesus so identifies with the hungry, thirsty, sick, destitute, downtrodden, and castoffs of the world that He regards acts of kindness and compassion done for them as being done for Him. In other words, whenever we serve the needy, we serve the King.

This is a mind-set that all of us who are Kingdom citizens need to develop. No person is beneath our dignity, unworthy of our compassion or beyond the reach of our love. We need to learn to look into the faces of other people and see the face of our King looking back at us. Regardless what our job, career, or profession, we have an assignment from our King to serve Him by serving others. That's why it is wrong for us to focus just on getting a paycheck or raising our standard of living. The paychecks will come, and so will greater prosperity, as long as we keep our focus where it ought to be: advancing the influence of the Kingdom by serving others in the King's name.

We are ambassadors of the King on a Kingdom mission. This understanding will ennoble any job, any undertaking, no matter how menial, unimportant, or even thankless it may seem from the human perspective. In the Kingdom of Heaven, no service is menial, unimportant, or thankless because the Kingdom is built on service.

THE LIFE OF A GOAT

Contrast all of this with the actions and attitude of the unrighteous, the "goats" at Jesus' left hand.

Then He will say to those on His left, "Depart from Me, you who are cursed, into the eternal fire prepared for the devil and his angels. For I was hungry and you gave Me nothing to eat, I was thirsty and you gave Me nothing to drink, I was a stranger and you did not invite Me in, I needed clothes and you did not clothe Me, I was sick and in prison and you did not look after Me."

They also will answer, "Lord, when did we see You hungry or thirsty or a stranger or needing clothes or sick or in prison and did not help You?"

He will reply, "I tell you the truth, whatever you did not do for one of the least of these, you did not do for Me."

Then they will go away to eternal punishment, but the righteous to eternal life" (Matthew 25:41-46).

From the Kingdom perspective, every person is either a sheep or a goat, either righteous or unrighteous, either a Kingdom citizen or an alien. It is important to note that the "goats" that the King addresses are not necessarily "bad" people. They may possess very high ethical and moral standards. In fact, they may very well be religious people. After all, they address the King as "Lord." And they seem genuinely surprised at the King's charge that they did nothing for Him: "Lord, when did we see You in need and not help You?" Implied in their question is the excuse, "Lord, if we had only known it was You, we would have acted differently." That's the whole point— and the fundamental difference between the sheep and the goats.

Unrighteous service is always calculated, always motivated by self-interest: "How will this benefit me in the long run?" Will it make you look good in front of your peers? Will it win you the praise of men? Will it bring you to the attention of the rich and powerful who can help you rise higher?

Righteous servants don't care about any of that. They treat everyone the same: rich or poor, strong or weak, lovely or unlovely, lovable or unlovable. To all they show the same love, demonstrate the same compassion and extend the same respect. Why? Because righteous servants are not after personal gain. All they are after is to obey and honor their King, whom they love with all their heart.

Serving others will not earn us a right standing with God. Righteous service is a by-product of a right standing with God. Right standing comes first and then service grows out of it. The ministry of righteous service is true Kingdom work. Apparently neither the sheep nor the goats recognized Jesus when He came to them in the guise of the broken, hurting, and needy. For the righteous it did not matter; they served lovingly and faithfully anyway, as serving their King.

Giving the Kingdom life to people can be an unconscious thing. The righteous asked, "Lord, when did we see You and do all these things for You?" For them it wasn't serving, it was life. God wants us to serve for no other reason than our love for Him and for other people. Some people serve because they want promotion. Some people serve because they want recognition. Some people serve because they want the applause of men. Some people serve because they want to gain some political, social, or economic advantage. The King wants our hearts to be so service-oriented that we serve without even thinking about it. Unconscious love is the best love in the world.

If you sit down and scheme as to whether or why to help a person, you are acting like a goat. Sheep ask, "How can I help?" while goats ask, "What's in it for me?" As Kingdom citizens, we should delight in the opportunity to serve. After all, we serve a King who came to earth to serve rather than be served, and when we serve willingly and joyfully in His name we do a very Kingly thing.

Service Reflects the Nature and Character of the Kingdom

Feed the hungry. Slake the thirsty. Welcome the stranger. Clothe the naked. Tend the sick. Visit the prisoner (or the infirm, bedridden or shut-in, as well as those who are psychologically or emotionally bound). These represent the very heart and soul of practical Kingdom life in this world. And yet these are the very same needs that most people fret and sweat and labor for all their lives. Can you see why Christ told us not to worry about these things? These things are the common currency, the *lingua franca* of the Kingdom. If we are actively pursuing Kingdom life, we live with these things every day. The King provides "all these things" to us so that we can be His instruments in providing them to others.

Service is not always easy. Some people are irritable, ungrateful, unlovely, and unlikable and would just as soon bite your head off as look at you. Sometimes people become so withdrawn and inwardly focused by the assaults of life that they seem to have no room in their heart or their perspective for anything other than themselves and their own personal grievances and complaints. Nevertheless, this does not excuse us from serving them with the same smile, the same love, and the same gentle and patient spirit we would give to others in need who were less difficult. After all, they too are created in the image of God.

Our eyes need to be alert to spot the strangers around us. I don't mean just people we don't know but also people who are strangers in society, people who are socially awkward or eccentric or painfully shy or lonely, people who may simply need a friend. It's always easier to care for people we know or like or who are most like us or who come from the same side of the tracks or who walk in the same socio-economic circles as we. But our calling as Kingdom citizens is to serve anyone and everyone with a need who crosses our path. We need to learn to regard such encounters not as random and unconnected events but as divine appointments providing us with the opportunity to share the love of God and introduce another person to His Kingdom.

What about new people at work? Do you welcome the new "strangers" in your office with a handshake and a smile? Do you try to set them at ease and help them get settled in or do you ignore them in resentment or fear that their arrival may mean your own job is in jeopardy?

Feed the hungry, satisfy the thirsty, clothe the naked; all of these evoke the image of people who lack the most basic human needs. Jesus said that the poor are with us always and that we can do something good for them any-time we choose (see Mark 14:7). The problem is that most of the time most of us choose to do nothing. Even worse, the poor are so ever-present that even if we do not turn our heads, we soon become so accustomed to their presence that we no longer see them, not even when we are looking right at them.

As Kingdom citizens positioned in righteousness, we have access to infinite provision for meeting the needs of the destitute. There is no excuse for us to turn our heads, pretend the poor are not there and blithely continue to consume Heaven's resources on our own greed and selfish desires.

Tend the sick. This one is a natural for those Kingdom citizens who are health-care professionals. Just be careful that you are not so professional that you lose the human touch. Even those of us who are not professionals in the health-care field can still tend the sick and hasten their healing by praying for them and by encouraging them through visits, phone calls, cards, child care, providing meals, and other such personal involvement.

Visit the prisoner. Prison inmates need ministry too. They need to experience the understanding and compassion of people who truly care about them and are willing to see them as people created in God's image and not just social misfits and outcasts.

There are other kinds of prisons too. Many people are imprisoned in their own homes because of fear, anxiety, or infirmity due to a body that is frail from sickness or no longer functions properly. These are often the forgotten ones in society: lonely, frightened, and depressed.

All of these needy ones are the kinds of people Jesus most identified with. He associated with them because

He loved them and because society, even the religious society, refused to do so. He is our King and sets our example. As He did we are to do also. That is what it means to be a Kingdom citizen. Service reflects the very nature and character of the Kingdom.

Service is powerful. In fact, service is the Kingdom's greatest ministry to humankind. When people of the world see Kingdom citizens in action, in humble yet joyful service, they see firsthand what the Kingdom of Heaven is like. Kingdom culture is so vastly different from worldly culture that seeing it on display in the lives of its citizens stirs up curiosity and even hunger for it in the hearts and minds of people who are outside the Kingdom. And this is just what God intends to happen. Hunger leads to inquiry and inquiry results in new Kingdom citizens.

True and faithful service also attracts the King's blessing. He says, "Because you serve Me well, I am going to give you the Kingdom. I will take care of your whole life. I will feed you, clothe you, provide a house and a car, and bless you with everything else you need to continue serving Me faithfully. Because of your faithfulness, I will give you the whole country."

Faithful service guarantees the Kingdom inheritance. Full access to the Kingdom and its resources is reserved for those who get their priorities right and put the Kingdom and righteousness of God ahead of their own desires, ambition, and comfort. There is nothing we can give up for the sake of the Kingdom that the King will not return to us multiplied many times over.

Service is the highest manifestation of Kingdom culture. The heart of the Kingdom of Heaven is the love of God and service is God's love in action from one human heart to another. And since God is love, service is also the King's nature in action. It is when we are busy feeding the hungry, giving water to the thirsty, welcoming the stranger, clothing the naked, tending the sick, and visiting the prisoner that we are most like our King.

THE MOTIVATIONS FOR GODLY SERVICE

There are two things that make the King's nature unique. One is love. God doesn't have love, and He doesn't give love. God is love. Love is His very nature. Love means a commitment and dedication to meet another person's needs above our own. It is this kind of love that took Jesus to the Cross to die for us while we were still sinners, still in rebellion against God. He did not wait for us to ask Him to die. He did it before we ever even knew to ask. He met our needs above His own.

Second, God's nature is caring. To care means to anticipate a need and meet it; planning to meet a need before it even arises. This is the nature of the King.

Because of the loving and caring nature of God, we as Kingdom citizens must always render service out of passion and not out of a desire or expectation of pay or any other kind of public or private acknowledgment. We must serve because we love it and because we love the King in whose name we serve. A popular aphorism says, "Do what you love and the money will follow." While that is certainly true, especially in the Kingdom, the Kingdom dynamic goes even farther: "Do what you love, whether the money follows or not." If you love living for the King and tending to His priorities, He will see to it that you never lack a thing.

Our service also must be motivated by love and not the limelight. Most of the work of service, including the most difficult work, takes place in secret, far from the public eye and the news media. If you thirst for the limelight, you will find the path of Kingdom service a very difficult road. Set your mind right now not to worry about the limelight. The King sees what you do in secret and His judgment is the only one that matters. So serve the King with a whole and undivided heart. Don't work for limelight. Work because you love God and because you love people.

Kingdom service proceeds from the revelation of the value of every human being as a unique creation in the image of God. It is very difficult to sustain a humble servant's heart over the long term if you cannot see the image of God in the face of every person you meet. Every person is entitled to basic dignity and respect. Remember, when you serve the needy, you serve the King.

Kingdom service is a calling, not a career. Careers are specialized according to education, preparation, and inclination, but every Kingdom citizen is called to be a servant. And that calling is for a lifetime. You can retire from a career, but you can't retire from a call. You can't retire from being yourself.

Service is the manifestation of the gifts God has given you. Work your gift, don't waste it. And the Bible says your gift will make room for you in the world.

PRINCIPLES

1. God's intent for us as Kingdom citizens is that we take on the culture of Heaven so that in whatever we do or say it will be evident that we belong to the Kingdom of Heaven.

2. The Kingdom of Heaven is our inheritance.

3. The government of God will last forever. His Kingdom is eternal.

4. We have a calling and a responsibility to influence earthly culture with the culture of Heaven.

5. Kingdom culture is a culture of servanthood.

6. In the Kingdom, you serve your way to greatness.

7. True servants live to serve and are delighted to do so.

8. Whenever we serve the needy, we serve the King.

9. Righteous service is a by-product of a right standing with God.

10. Our calling as Kingdom citizens is to serve anyone and everyone with a need who crosses our path.

11. Service reflects the very nature and character of the Kingdom.

12. Kingdom service is a calling, not a career.

"He who sells fruit never advertises the tree."

CHAPTER ELEVEN

THE PROCESS OF
ENTERING THE KINGDOM

The most important part of the Kingdom experience is the process of entering the Kingdom. Unless you know how to get into the Kingdom of Heaven, everything else about the Kingdom is meaningless. What do you do to enter the Kingdom of God, and how does it work? To answer these two questions, let me begin with an illustration involving my own country.

The number one industry in the Bahamas is tourism. Every year our tiny island nation of 300,000 people hosts over 5 million tourists. This means that tourists outnumber residents by a factor of almost 17 to 1. Tourism alone brings in over $1 billion of revenue each year. Ours is the most successful tourism nation in our entire region of the Caribbean. No other country in the region receives the number of tourists that we receive in these small islands.

Why is the Bahamas so successful? To get more to the point, why don't people around the world come to Jesus and to the Kingdom of God the way they come to the Bahamas? Why aren't there 5 million people coming into the church every year? Why are they more excited about coming to the Bahamas than coming to God? Why are they willing to spend an average of $200 per night per room, excluding taxes, for an average of about $1,500 a week for a couple? Why would they give that kind of money to us? What brings them here?

The reason for our success, the reason why we have 5 million tourists coming to the Bahamas every year, is because we do not advertise or promote the prime minister. If you want people to come to your country, you don't advertise the government. You don't brag about how good the prime minister is, or the president. People do not visit the Bahamas because of our prime minister.

SELL THE COUNTRY!

Why is this so important? It goes back to what Jesus said in Matthew 6:33, that we should seek first the Kingdom and righteousness of God. The Kingdom is God's greatest priority and Jesus said there are some great benefits that will be added free to all who set their minds to seek the Kingdom above all other priorities.

I think it is highly significant that before Jesus invited us to enter the Kingdom, He told us about its benefits. He said, "Why do you worry about what you will eat or drink or wear?" He dealt first with our primary interests, the things that drive us through life from day to day. He said, "Your heavenly Father knows you need food, water, clothing, and shelter. He knows exactly what you are after, your every need and every desire of your heart. Don't worry, all of those things are in His Kingdom."

I'm going to step out on a theological limb here, so please read very carefully: Jesus never said, *"Seek Me first."* He said, *"Seek first the Kingdom."* If we put our prime minister's photograph, biography, and personal profile on all of our tourism advertisements, no one will come to the Bahamas. That's not to say anything against the prime minister, but that is not what the tourists are interested in. They don't want to know about the government or the political leadership; they want to know about the country. If we want to attract tourists to the Bahamas, we need to tell them and show them things about our country that will whet their appetite and stir up in them the desire to come visit.

Jesus never told us to seek Him first. And yet the church, for the better part of its 2,000- year history, has done precisely that. The church continuously has preached about the King, and taught about the King, and bragged about the King, and told people how they should love the King, and give their hearts to the King, and follow the King, and serve the King, and live for the King. And while all of this is true, it is probably not the best place to start, because in all the talk and attention given to the King, very little focus has been given to the Kingdom He reigns over.

If you want to attract people to your country, you have to show them how and why your country is better than theirs; prove to them that they can get benefits in your country that they cannot get in their own. The church keeps talking only about Jesus and not about the Kingdom (which is what He told us to talk about), and then wonders why so few people are interested.

There are 1.2 billion Muslims in the world and they all need Jesus. But they are not interested. Hindus world-wide number 600 million and counting, and they all need Jesus. But they are not interested. Why? Because people aren't interested in the head of state. Tell them about the country. Get them excited about the country and its benefits. Then, when they ask how to get in, tell them about Jesus. Tell them that the King is the doorway into the country. Then they will be interested in the King.

We don't advertise the Bahamas with pictures or information about the prime minister or other public officials. Quite often our promotional materials show no people at all, just sun, blue tropical waters, white sand, green coconut palm trees, and beautiful red hibiscus in December! Can you imagine how enticing an image that is for Canadians or northern Americans snowed in by four-foot drifts? That's why they come here. That's why one of the largest and fastest growing industries in the Bahamas right now is external owners of property. People all over the world want to live here. Why? It's not because of the prime minister; he'll be replaced in a few years.

People want to move here because here is better than where they are—beach living with an average temperature of 75 degrees year-round. We sell them on an ocean filled with pure, fresh, clean fish and no pollution. We sell them on warm hospitality and good-looking people with positive attitudes. We don't sell them the prime minister. Here's the bottom line. The secret to attracting visitors or investors or new citizens is to promise them the lifestyle, the benefits, and the environment of the country.

This is why people are not coming to God. We keep trying to sell them on the leader. Jesus never preached Himself to the multitudes. He preached the Kingdom of Heaven. He taught the Kingdom of Heaven. He used every example and word-picture He could to show the people what the Kingdom is like. On one occasion He compared the Kingdom of Heaven to a wedding feast a king gave for his son (see Matt. 22:1-14). Try to imagine what a feast like that would be like: landscaped grounds, full, beautiful trees, gold carpets, silver walls, silver spoons, golden goblets, all the food you can eat, grapes, wine, cheese, fresh meat! Wow! If that's what the Kingdom of Heaven is like, don't you want to go there? I know I do! That's selling the country.

Jesus Christ is not the Kingdom; He is the King. He is also the Door into the Kingdom. Anyone who wishes to enter the Kingdom of Heaven must go in through the Door, which is Jesus. But you don't draw people to your country by talking about the port of entry. You draw them by selling them on what lies beyond the port of entry—the country's benefits and quality of life—by stirring up such a hunger and desire for the country that they will do anything to get in.

Jesus said, "*The Law and the Prophets were proclaimed until John. Since that time, the good news of the kingdom of God is being preached, and everyone is forcing his way into it*" (Luke 16:16). Why aren't people forcing their way into Christianity? They don't want Christianity because Christianity is built on a door, not on the Kingdom beyond the door. Muslims don't want Jesus. They are satisfied with Muhammad and Allah. But talk to them about the Kingdom of Heaven and its riches, abundance, prosperity, and joy, as well as a Personal God who loves them, and compare that to the barren austerity in which most Muslims live, and you may get a listening ear.

People really are not looking for Jesus. We keep telling them they are but they are not. They are looking for things. They are looking for a good life. But open their eyes to the reality of the Kingdom and their focus will change. Who wouldn't trade the rat race pursuit of things for a Kingdom that guarantees all those things free and without frustration? That's what Jesus meant when He said people were forcing their way into the Kingdom of God. Once a person understands what the Kingdom is, and the riches, benefits, and joys it affords, he or she will do anything to get in, even risk life and limb. Why is it that more and more Muslims are converting to Christ even though they know it may cost them their lives? Because they have discovered the Kingdom of Heaven and have realized that no price is too great to pay to enter it.

THE PRIORITY OF GOD FOR HUMANKIND

According to Jesus, the most important priority for people on earth is the Kingdom of Heaven. The Kingdom of Heaven is the most important thing on earth. It is the treasure, the pearl, the yeast, the light, and the salt of the earth. The Kingdom is everything. Jesus nailed this point home with two related parables:

The kingdom of Heaven is like treasure hidden in a field. When a man found it, he hid it again, and then in his joy went and sold all he had and bought that field. Again, the kingdom of Heaven is like a merchant looking for fine pearls. When he found one of great value, he went away and sold everything he had and bought it (Matthew 13:44-46).

Jesus said that the Kingdom of Heaven is like treasure that is so precious and so valuable that it is worth giving up everything else just to possess it. Throughout the ages countless people have left their homes and families, traveled all over the world, endured incredible hardship, and risked death and disaster daily, drawn by the lure of treasure and riches. It is amazing how much people are willing to risk on even the smallest chance of striking pay dirt.

Jesus said that's the way we are supposed to be about the Kingdom. We are supposed to pursue it even to and through the point of personal danger because once we enter it we've got it made. If we are willing to take such chances for earthly treasure that will eventually pass away, how much more willing should we be to risk everything for the sake of gaining the Kingdom.

Likewise, the Kingdom of Heaven is like a precious pearl that a merchant found and then sold everything he had to buy it. That's how precious the Kingdom is. It is worth any price. Apparently the merchant had nothing left after buying the pearl except the pearl, and that was enough. So it is with the Kingdom. When we have the Kingdom, that is enough. Everything is in the Kingdom. We don't need anything else.

THE PRIORITY OF JESUS

Jesus' only priority on earth was the Kingdom of Heaven. He taught us that the Kingdom should be our highest priority also, even in our prayers:

This, then, is how you should pray: "Our Father in Heaven, hallowed be Your name, Your kingdom come, Your will be done on earth as it is in Heaven" (Matthew 6:9-10).

Notice that Jesus says that this is how we should pray. *We* should pray for God's Kingdom to come on earth. *We* should pray for His will to be done. He never says that we should pray for *Him* to come. Yet that is just what the church has prayed for centuries. Jesus will return one day and it will be a blessed day when He does, but that is not how He told us to pray. The focus of our prayers should be that the Kingdom of Heaven should come, that the influence of Heaven's government should permeate the nations and cultures of the earth like yeast in dough.

In Luke's account of Jesus' last supper with His disciples the night before He was crucified, Jesus says at one point, *"I confer on you a kingdom, just as my Father conferred one on Me"* (Luke 22:29). That is a political statement. Every government, when appointing ambassadors, uses the word "confer."

When I received my medals from the Queen of England, I stood in that wonderful place of dignity with all the other people being so honored. When my moment came, I knelt, a sword was placed on my shoulder, and the official holding the sword said to me, "I confer on you the OBE award of the kingdom of Great Britain." When I stood up, I was a different person. They called me an OBE (for Order of the British Empire). I went down as a simple Bahamian citizen and rose up as an OBE. In those few seconds they conferred on me the whole empire. The Queen of England has the power to give me her kingdom.

Hanging on the wall in my office is the OBE citation with my name on it and bearing Queen Elizabeth's signature and the royal seal. Because I am now an OBE, I automatically receive special honor and preferential treatment whenever I travel anywhere in the Commonwealth of Great Britain or in any of the nations formerly in the Commonwealth. It is not me they are honoring so much as the kingdom because when I walk into a place wearing my OBE medal, the kingdom goes in with me.

When I was named an OBE, in effect the entire country was conferred on me.

That is what Jesus did for us with the Kingdom of Heaven. He conferred the Kingdom on us. The Kingdom is Jesus' top priority and it must be ours as well.

Religion postpones the Kingdom to a future experience, which is why you don't hear much about the Kingdom in religion. You cannot appropriate what you postpone. If you say the Kingdom is coming later, you can never experience it now. However, God's desire is for you to enter and experience the Kingdom *right now.*

ENTERING THE KINGDOM

The number one goal of all humanity should be to enter the Kingdom. But what does it mean to enter the Kingdom? This is a very important question because most of us have been taught that entering the Kingdom means dying and going to Heaven. This is not true. Whenever Jesus uses the word enter with reference to the Kingdom, He is not referring to dying and going anywhere. He is talking about entering into the lifestyle of the Kingdom. When you enter the Kingdom you begin to experience the life of the country.

To enter also means to pursue and attain citizenship in the Kingdom of Heaven. Citizenship inherits everything in the Kingdom. When you become a citizen, you have privileges and rights to everything in the constitution.

So make the Kingdom of Heaven your priority and get into it.

For better understanding of entering the Kingdom, let's consider three statements that Jesus made. First, "*I tell you the truth, unless you change and become like little children, you will never enter the kingdom of heaven*" (Matt. 18:3). Jesus did not say, "Unless you die, you will not enter," but "*unless you change and become like little children you will not enter*." Why did He use the simile of little children? Because children simply submit to their environment. They go along with whatever they see. In innocence a child will play with a snake or move toward a flame because the child doesn't know any better. The child simply submits to the environment and assumes everything is safe.

When Jesus said we should become like little children, He was saying that when we come into the Kingdom we should just live like we're in it. Accept it on childlike faith. Submit to its influence, its mandate, its values, its morals, its standards, its dictates. Obey its laws and follow its principles.

The difference between a child and an adult is that a child obeys and an adult negotiates. Jesus is saying, "Be like a child. Don't try to negotiate with me. If I tell you to stop sinning, stop sinning. It's that simple."

Jesus' second statement is one He spoke to a rich young man who asked Him what to do to receive eternal life: "*There is only one who is good. If you want to enter life, obey the commandments"* (Matt. 19:17b). If you want to come to the Bahamas and enjoy our good Bahamian life, you must abide by our Bahamian law or else you may end up cooling your heels in our nice Bahamian jail. By the same token, if you want to enter Kingdom living and experience Kingdom lifestyle you must obey Kingdom laws. Otherwise you may find yourself cut off from Kingdom resources and bowing under Kingdom judgment.

Jesus made the third statement right after the rich young man went away sad because he was unable to part with his wealth in order to follow Jesus: *"I tell you the truth, it is hard for a rich man to enter the kingdom of Heaven"* (Matt. 19:23b). Here Jesus is not talking about initial entrance into the Kingdom. He's talking about experiencing it. Why? Because in the Kingdom, the King owns everything. If you come into the Kingdom through the new birth in Christ but do not surrender your mindset of ownership, you will be unable to experience the fullness of Kingdom life because you are trying to hoard instead of releasing.

Kingdom citizenship can be prevented by religion. In fact, according to Jesus, religion is the most dangerous opponent to Kingdom citizenship. Jesus had many run-ins with the teachers of the law and the Pharisees, the religious leaders of His day; because they, by their own actions, were keeping many people out of the Kingdom.

"Woe to you, teachers of the law and Pharisees, you hypocrites! You shut the kingdom of Heaven in men's

faces. You yourselves do not enter, nor will you let those enter who are trying to" (Matt. 23:13).

Religion can prevent Kingdom life because religion pretends to be a substitute. Anyone who thinks the substitute is the real thing will miss out on the real thing. Unfortunately, there are many people trapped in "religious" Christianity who believe that what they have is all there is, yet they know next to nothing about the Kingdom. They cannot enter into something they know nothing about.

Once when I was leading a conference in southern Florida, a pastor came up to me and said, "So, you're the Kingdom preacher, huh?"

I replied, "And you're not?"

He became very quiet. Finally, he asked, "What do you mean?"

"Come," I said, "let's sit down and have a cup of tea." We sat down together and I took my Bible and began showing him Scripture after Scripture about the Kingdom. He wept. Then he asked if I would join him after the evening session. I agreed.

At 2 o'clock in the morning he was still asking me questions. "Where did you learn all this?"

"From the same book you use, that Bible right in front of you."

"Well, how come no one ever showed me?"

243

I said, "God only shows you what you want to see. Religion blinds you."

He fell on his knees before me right there in the restaurant. "Pray for me," he said. "I want forgiveness. I've been a pastor for 37 years and I've been preaching the wrong message. Pray for me."

I laid my hands on him and prayed for him. He got up, went to the book table and bought one of everything. He said, "I'm starting over."

"No," I said, "you are finally entering yourself."

Watch out for religion. It can keep you from experiencing the fullness of Kingdom life.

THE PROCESS TO CITIZENSHIP

Jesus explained the process of acquiring Kingdom citizenship during a dead-of-night meeting with a leading Pharisee named Nicodemus. Their conversation is recorded in the Gospel of John chapter 3. This is the only place in the Bible where the words born again are found, and Jesus uses those words in describing to Nicodemus the process of becoming a Kingdom citizen.

Nicodemus had heard Jesus teach numerous times and so had certainly heard Him speak about the Kingdom. But Nicodemus did not understand the teaching even though he was a highly educated expert in the Jewish law. Nevertheless, he was intrigued by both Jesus' manner and message and wanted to know more. So he came secretly by night to inquire of Jesus.

Now there was a man of the Pharisees named Nicodemus, a member of the Jewish ruling council. He came to Jesus at night and said, "Rabbi, we know that you are a teacher who has come from God. For no one could perform the miraculous signs You are doing if God were not with Him."

In reply Jesus declared, "I tell you the truth, no one can see the kingdom of God unless he is born again."

"How can a man be born when he is old?" Nicodemus asked. "Surely he cannot enter a second time into his mother's womb to be born!"

Jesus answered, "I tell you the truth, no one can enter the kingdom of God unless he is born of water and the Spirit. Flesh gives birth to flesh, but the Spirit gives birth to spirit. You should not be surprised at My saying, 'You must be born again.' The wind blows wherever it pleases. You hear its sound, but you cannot tell where it comes from or where it is going. So it is with everyone born of the Spirit" (John 3:1-8).

Here was Nicodemus, a respected religious leader, asking Jesus, an itinerant rabbi from Galilee, how to enter the Kingdom of God. Nicodemus would never have asked such a question or sought such a thing as the Kingdom unless he had found his strict religious observances unsatisfying. Jesus' teachings on the Kingdom had stirred in Nicodemus a hunger for more than he was experiencing. He was at the top of the Judaic religious ladder and knew he was not where he wanted to be. He wanted to be in Jesus' country. He wanted to know how to become a citizen of the Kingdom of God.

Let's look closely at Jesus' answer, because so often we have misunderstood His words. He said, "*No one can see the kingdom of God unless he is born again.*" The Greek word for see in this verse means "to experience, or to understand." Jesus was telling Nicodemus, "You can neither understand nor experience Kingdom life unless you are born into the country." This is not a religious statement.

I was born in the Bahamas; I didn't have to become a citizen. I was a citizen by birth. Anyone not born in the Bahamas who wants to become a citizen has to go through a long and complicated process. In this regard, God's Kingdom operates a little differently from other countries. God's Kingdom has no citizenship "process." Either you're born again or you aren't. Once you are born again, your citizenship "process" is instantaneous.

Upon hearing the necessity of being born again, Nicodemus asked a very logical question: "How can a man be born when he is old?" Did Nicodemus misunderstand Jesus? No. His question proves it. This is an important point. Jesus literally told Nicodemus that he had to be born again the way he was born the first time. There was no spiritual or theological confusion. Jesus said, "The way you become a citizen of My country is the same way you become a citizen in any other country. You have to be born into citizenship."

"OK," Nicodemus answered, "but I'm an old man. Do I have to go back and be a baby again and enter a woman's womb and be born all over?" Another logical question because he had heard a logical answer. Nicodemus understood Jesus' reference to being born again as referring to a natural birth, and he was correct. There are no illegal immigrants in the Kingdom of God, and no illegitimate children, either. Every Kingdom citizen is a bona fide native-born citizen.

But how can this be? Like Nicodemus, none of us can reverse time, become babies again, and return to our mother's womb for rebirth. If birth into the Kingdom of God is a natural birth, how does it happen?

Jesus said, "No one can enter the Kingdom of God unless he is born of water and the Spirit. This is good news for every one of us! No matter who or where we are, God has made special governmental arrangements for us literally to be born citizens in the Kingdom of Heaven legally. Flesh gives birth to flesh, He says. In the same way we were born physically, the Spirit gives birth to spirit. Jesus says, "I have made arrangements for my country to give you a new birth spiritually." That's why He says we *must* be born again. He's talking about citizenship rights.

Natural citizenship is a result of natural birth. And so the Kingdom of Heaven is a "super natural" other-worldly Kingdom, which is why heavenly Kingdom citizenship requires heavenly Kingdom spiritual birth. Jesus has made arrangements for every one of us to be born spiritually and to achieve supernatural citizenship in the Kingdom of God. When? Now. If you are born again, you are a Kingdom citizen right now, and all the rights, benefits, and privileges of citizenship are yours right now.

RECEIVING THE NEW BIRTH

If you have not been born again, that is the step you must take before you can become a Kingdom citizen and receive eternal life. This is why Jesus came. He came not only as the one who announced the coming of the Kingdom, but also as the one through whom we gain entrance to the Kingdom: *"For God so loved the world that He gave His one and only Son, that whoever believes in Him shall not perish but have eternal life"* (John 3:16).

Receiving the new birth is not a difficult process.

1. Acknowledge that you are a sinner in rebellion against God: *"For all have sinned and fall short of the glory of God"* (Rom. 3:23).

2. Understand that the penalty for sin is eternal death: *"For the wages of sin is death, but the gift of God is eternal life in Christ Jesus our Lord"* (Rom. 6:23).

3. Believe that Jesus Christ died for your sins so that you might be forgiven: *"But God demonstrates His own love for us in this: While we were still sinners, Christ died for us"* (Rom. 5:8).

4. Confess your sins to God: *"If we confess our sins, He is faithful and just and will forgive us our sins and purify us from all unrighteousness"* (1 John 1:9). To confess your sins means to agree with God regarding your sins.

5. Repent of your sins: *"Unless you repent, you too will all perish"* (Luke 13:3). To repent means to make a clean break with sin, a 180-degree reversal of direction.

6. Confess Christ as your Savior and Lord and give Him control of your life: *"If you confess with your mouth, 'Jesus is Lord,' and believe in your heart that God raised Him from the dead, you will be saved. For it is with your heart that you believe and are justified, and it is with your mouth that you confess and are saved"* (Rom. 10:9-10).

THE SECRET OF CONCEPTION

When I was born in the Bahamas, one of the first things they did was put ink on my foot and pressed it onto a piece of paper. That footprint, along with my name and official registration, was filed at the hospital and a copy sent to the registrar general downtown as a record that mine was a registered birth in the Bahamas. If anyone wants to know where I was born, all he has to do is check the registry. Most other countries follow a similar procedure.

Conception is a secret process invisible to the naked eye. When you and I were conceived, nobody was watching, probably, except God. In other words, when the process of birth began, it was secret. Jesus said that the new birth is like the wind; no one can see it. Likewise, citizenship is not a visual reality but a disposition.

In John 3:8 Jesus says, *"The wind blows wherever it pleases. You hear its sound, but you cannot tell where it comes from or where it is going. So it is with everyone born of the Spirit."* When you give your life or surrender your life to the King and He gives you a new birth, no one sees that. It may happen at an altar, in the back of a car, at home, at school; wherever you receive Christ, the process is invisible. The new birth involves believing, and no one can see you believing. Belief, like conception, is invisible.

Sometimes the new birth is accompanied by a feeling and sometimes it isn't. Everybody is different, so everybody's response to the new birth will be different. Feeling something is not the point. The point is that spiritual conception took place and internal change is underway. When a woman conceives, her clothes don't change. She doesn't even realize until some time later that something is going on.

The same thing happens spiritually. When you're born again, you surrender to Christ. Some weeks later it suddenly dawns on you that you don't enjoy sin anymore. That's change. That's a sign of the new birth. You have been born again. That's why it's impossible now for you to sin and feel the same way about it as you once did.

In fact, sin eventually becomes a terror to you. Why? Because that is not your nature anymore. You've been born from above. And your Kingdom citizenship began the moment you were born again.

PRINCIPLES

1. Unless you know how to get into the Kingdom of Heaven, everything else about the Kingdom is meaningless.

2. Jesus never said, *"Seek Me first."* He said, *"Seek first the Kingdom."*

3. The most important priority of people on earth is the Kingdom of Heaven.

4. When we have the Kingdom, that is enough.

5. God's desire is for you to enter and experience the Kingdom right now.

6. When you enter the Kingdom, you begin to experience the life of the country.

7. Kingdom citizenship can be prevented by religion.

8. You can neither understand nor experience Kingdom life unless you are born into the country.

9. Once you are born again, your citizenship "process" is instantaneous.

10. God has made special governmental arrangements for us literally to be born citizens in the Kingdom of Heaven legally.

11. The new birth involves believing, and no one can see you believing. Belief, like conception, is invisible.

12. Your Kingdom citizenship began the moment you were born again.

Bahamas
Faith Ministries
International

The Diplomat Center
Carmichael Road
P.O. Box N-9583
Nassau, Bahamas

TEL: (242) 341-6444
FAX (242) 361-2260

Website:
http://www.bfmmm.com

Additional copies of this book and other
book titles from DESTINY IMAGE are
available at your local bookstore.

For a bookstore near you, call 1-800-722-6774.

Send a request for a catalog to:

Destiny Image® Publishers, Inc.

P.O. Box 310
Shippensburg, PA 17257-0310

"Speaking to the Purposes of God for this
Generation and for the Generations to Come"

For a complete list of our titles,
visit us at www.destinyimage.com